DHUODA

NINTH CENTURY MOTHER AND THEOLOGIAN

DHUODA

NINTH CENTURY MOTHER AND THEOLOGIAN

Marie Anne Mayeski

Scranton: University of Scranton Press

BV
4596
.P75
D4835
1995

Marketing and Distribution
Fordham University Press
University Box L
Bronx NY 10458

PRINTED IN THE UNITED STATES OF AMERICA

To Robert E. McNally, S.J. (1917-1977)

Mentor and Friend.

CONTENTS

Abbreviations   ix

Acknowlededements   xi

Introduction   1

1. Dhuoda in Historical Context   9

2. Dhuoda in Theological Context   37

3. The Syro-Phoenician Woman   65

4. The Beatitudes and the Moral Life of the Christian   93

5. Biblical Wisdom: Obedience and Conflict of Loyalties   117

Conclusion   140

Appendices   145

Bibliography   161

Indices   169

ABBREVIATIONS

ACW	Ancient Christian Writers.
ANF	Ante-Nicene Fathers.
CC	Corpus Christianorum, Series Latina.
DDC	Augustine, *De Doctrina Christiana.*
DVV	Alcuin, *De Vitiis Et Virtutibus.*
Ephem Lit	*Ephémerides Liturgiensis.*
HGL	Histoire Générale de Languedoc.
LCC	Library of Christian Classics.
MGH	Monumenta Germaniae Historica.
NCE	*New Catholic Encyclopedia.*
NPNF	Nicene and Post Nicene Fathers.
PL	Patrologia Latina.
RAM	Revue d'ascétique et de mystique.
RB	*Revue Benedictine.*
REAug	*Revue des études augustiniennes.*
RecTh	*Recherches de théologie ancienne et médiévale.*
SC	Sources Chrétiennes.
SCH	*Studies in Church History.*
SL	Studia Liturgica.
TS	Theological Studies.

ACKNOWLEDGEMENTS

This project grew slowly and over a long period of time. The list of those to whom I am indebted is proportionately long. I must, first of all, acknowledge the help and competence of the library staff of the Von der Ahe Library at Loyola Marymount University, especially Christine Anderson and Anthony Amodeo. They and their staff significantly enlarged the resources of our modest collection through interlibrary loan and various electronic bibliographic searches.

Loyola Marymount University contributed financial support through its Summer Research Grant Program and the Chilton Chair. The summer stipends provided me with the opportunity to write two of the chapters which appear here. I am particularly grateful to the College of Liberal Arts and to its dean, Mary Milligan, RSHM, for giving me the College Fellowship in spring, 1994, allowing me the time necessary to complete the manuscript.

Various colleagues read pieces of this work in progress. Jeffrey Siker, Lizette Larson-Miller, Daniel Christopher, Randall Cummings, James Fredericks, S.S., Jane Crawford and Susan Rabe were generous with their time and their constructive criticism. Any flaws in the text remain my own but without the support and assistance of these wonderful friends and scholars, this work could not have come to completion.

A special word of thanks belongs to two people who helped me with technical assistance. My brother, Simon Mayeski, introduced me to the complexities and possibilities of the computer at the beginning of this project and patiently endured lengthy telephone calls whenever I got lost in the intricacies of word-processing. Beatrice Henson-O'Neal, Administrative Secretary of the

Marymount Institute for Faith, Culture and the Arts helped enormously with the technical details of completing the manuscript. Her patience, diligence and expertise deserve more eloquent praise than I can offer here.

INTRODUCTION

In a recent article in *Theological Studies*, Randy L. Maddox from Sioux Falls College in South Dakota notes that "calls for recovering . . . an understanding of theology as a practical discipline have become increasingly common in recent years."[1] His sources document that increased interest, particularly among German scholars whose disciplinary concern is theological method. Other evidence supports Maddox's observation. Certainly liberation theology, feminist theology and other political theologies have issued a clarion call for a theological study that is rooted and results in life and action. Using such words as 'malaise' and 'recovery' to express the dissatisfaction of many for whom theology is a matter of interest, Maddox suggests that theology served both its practitioners and its audiences better in an earlier time. His historical analysis is not a romantic panegyric in praise of any particular age, but a demonstration of the particular nature of theology from the earliest days until the twelfth century. During that time, says Maddox, theology was understood, first of all, as a "*habitus* of the believer, a cognitive and affectional disposition or orientation toward God, others, and creation" (651). Its secondary meaning was that "discipline of study, instruction, and pastoring directed toward forming" that *habitus* in believers. Maddox notes that this early understanding conceived of theology as a single discipline, in which all aspects of faith and life formed a coherent whole. He does not underline, though he might have done so, that the Bible was the primary text of these early theologians; he does insist that the social setting of the practice of theology—at first, the bishop's parish congregation and then, the monastery—was both

---

[1] "The Recovery of Theology as a Practical Discipline," *Theological Studies* 51 (1990): 650.

evidence of its practical nature and a shaping force in its development.

Maddox credits, or discredits, Aquinas with solidifying the shift of theology from a practical to a speculative discipline, which was newly situated in a world apart, the university. Gradually, practical theology became spiritual theology, a secondary exercise designed to provide grist for the mills of the devotional lives of the faithful. The subsequent history of theology, as told by Maddox, is the story of a discipline that became more and more the preserve of philosophical experts, separated both by their concerns and their location from the lives of the faithful, while practical theology became ever more narrowly focused on the technical aspects of ministerial formation. Maddox calls for a recovery of theology as a practical discipline as he identifies five characteristics that such a renewed theology must have: 1) the reunification of the various branches of theology into a common concern for practice; 2) the concentration of the various goals of theology into a unified attempt to shape the character of believers; 3) the recovery of praxis as the ultimate goal of theological activity; 4) a renewed emphasis on the power of theological reflection to transform life; 5) the reintegration of the theological process into the community of faith.

Writing from the perspective of the biblical scholar, Sandra M. Schneiders raises critical questions that intersect with Maddox's analysis. In *The Revelatory Text*, she asserts that contemporary biblical scholarship has been so exclusively concerned with the historical critical method that it has failed to develop a hermeneutical theory.[2] In her own words, "[biblical scholarship] knows *how* to do what it is doing, but has uncritically taken for granted that *what* it is doing is exactly and only what needs to be done in order for this text . . . to be truly understood.[3] She points out that "a chorus of discordant voices from the periphery of the

---

[2] (San Francisco: Harper, 1991), 21–25.

[3] p. 21.

field" (21) has raised questions that the historical critical exegetes cannot answer; the chorus includes those whose fields are sociology, psychology, and liberationist theory as well as those who search for a "spiritually fruitful understanding of Scripture" (23). Schneiders' work is "a serious engagement of the theological and ecclesial claims made for the Bible" (25). As such, it can be understood as part of the process of "recovery" for which Maddox and others have called. To recover an earlier mode of doing theology and biblical study is not, of course, to ignore the accomplishments of modern scholarship but to reclaim the Bible as the church's book and theology as the scholarly discourse about the full life of the church, its doctrine and theory as well as its liturgical, political and moral practice.

This task of recovery can also be nourished by the kind of historical study on which Maddox builds his argument. Certainly the theological study of medieval texts has often been impeded by academic attitudes formed by the post-scholastic history Maddox narrates. Such texts have often been relegated to the category of "mere" devotional texts, particularly if they were written by women and others without academic status. Judged through the prism of a certain philosophical theological method, they have been found "unsystematic." Their use of the biblical text has been dismissed as "precritical." Even when contemporary scholars have praised such a precritical understanding,[4] their use of such terminology gives the impression that medieval exegetes and theologians were uncritical and arbitrary, without clear norms for determining a valid meaning of the text. Certain medieval texts have been valued, of course, if they are shown to have influenced later, more sophisticated theologians, though to the extent that they have themselves been influenced by the earlier tradition, they are often considered merely derivative. Perhaps, however, the criteria for practical theology, offered by Maddox, can provide a new lens

---

[4] See, for instance, David C. Steinmetz, "The Superiority of Pre-Critical Exegesis," *Theology Today* 37 (1980): 27–38.

through which to view the accomplishments of some early medieval theologians. Then we would ask, for instance, how unified was the medieval author's view of the mystery? How was the biblical text read in connection with the circumstances of the author's life? What methods of biblical interpretation pertained? How did praxis flow from doctrine and vice versa? How well tailored was the theological reflection to the specific characteristics of the life of the intended audience? What understanding of human nature guided the author and how was the transformation of that nature understood? What kind of life and practice was held out as the goal of such transformation? How was character formation presented? Such questions can change our perspectives on a wide range of medieval texts.

The absence of a hermeneutical framework such as this has, I believe, hampered a genuine, theological understanding of early medieval texts. The history of the recent appropriation of one such text may be instructive: the *Liber Manualis* was written by Dhuoda of Septimania, a Carolingian aristocrat, for the practical and religious formation of her sons. The discovery of a third manuscript was the beginning of a new scholarly interest in this text, which had previously been of interest only to the regional historians of Nîmes and its environs, the original provenance of the work. Pierre Riché, S.J., of the University of Paris undertook the important task of editing the three extant manuscripts and published a critical edition in *SC* in 1975. At first, the new edition excited the interest primarily of prosopographical scholars. Others in the area of social history began to plumb the work and feminist historians such as Suzanne Wemple found evidence therein to support a growing understanding of the actual lives of aristocratic women in the ninth century. Peter Dronke included a literary analysis of Dhuoda's work in his *Women Writers of the Medieval Period*. Most recently, an excellent English translation by Carol Neel has appeared which, with its introduction and notes, has made the text accessible to students in a variety of disciplines.

Though a scattering of essays have been published which hold up a theological lens to Dhuoda's work, there is still much to be done. Her work can best be understood, I think, in the context of exegetical and hermeneutical history. For it is the Bible, read as a whole and understood as the sweeping story of salvation, which holds together the various pieces of practical advice which Dhuoda offers to her son and his companions. She appropriates the Bible with the full play of methods at her disposal, methods based on liturgical typology and allegory as well as on grammatical studies. The Bible is, for her, the framework and narrative of her own story and that of her family. Sometimes, therefore, her exegesis is personal, an explication of her own personal history; at other times, it is exegesis for the particular community of aristocratic leaders among whom her older son is taking his place. In both cases, her understanding of doctrinal truth is orthopractic; never inclined to speculation, she tests the truth of Scripture by its relevance to the practical decisions which face her, her family and their peers. Her hermeneutic presuppositions, as well as many of her particular interpretations, are traditional, but they are always recast in the categories and language of her own day and class.

In studying Dhuoda's *Liber Manualis* from the perspective of exegetical history, therefore, we can broaden and enrich our present understanding of the complex world of early medieval exegesis. Certain unique aspects make Dhuoda's text especially appropriate to this task. As a laywoman, Dhuoda's work demonstrates that the "theology of the people" was not greatly distanced from that of the professionals. It is not "popular" if that word is taken to mean a theology generated from a level of experience not shared by the clerical and monastic leadership or by court theologians. It is, rather, informed by the same texts and understood by the same methods utilized by those better-known medieval writers. The issues are not substantially different from the ones addressed by those in high places. Dhuoda has her own version of the conviction that "all politics are local;" for her, all the theological and moral issues raised by the theocracy in which she lives are personal and familial. For this reason, perhaps, Dhuoda's text is more personal in its self-revelation than are the general run of texts by bishops, abbots and court theologians. But, for all of its intimacy, it remains a theological work, written to communicate an orthodox and comprehensive understanding of the mystery of salvation experienced anew within a specific social and political situation.

Dhuoda's exegetical and theological work in crafting the *Liber Manualis* is the subject of this book. After a contextual chapter, in which I position Dhuoda within the appropriate historical and literary framework, it is necessary to expose her hermeneutics; this involves a discussion of her presuppositions and the various methods of biblical interpretation she employs. In three separate chapters, I show Dhuoda employing these various methods in the pursuance of three theological tasks. In the first case, she uses a small bit of New Testament text allusively in order to substantiate her self-identity as theologian; a fairly straight-forward reading of herself into the text allows us to see the intimate connection between text and reader that was important to all early medieval theology. It also demonstrates the subtlety and care with which historical texts were enlarged to include the stories of later believers, not arbitrarily but through the refined application of grammatical and typological methods.

In the second instance, we see Dhuoda re-working a popular moral tradition based on the beatitudes into a developmental program appropriate to an adolescent warrior. This task involves, on the one hand, an understanding of the theological reasoning by which biblical text became developed doctrine and, on the other, a magisterial freedom in reworking established doctrine according to the social realities of its new audience. Her development of the beatitude tradition also demonstrates Dhuoda's understanding of the role played by psychological and social development in preparing for the reception of doctrine. In her third task, Dhuoda undertakes to develop a moral strategy by which a young warrior can negotiate the various and often conflicting claims upon his loyalty. This requires that she construct a theological understanding of the social order in which she may then articulate the political role of royal counsellor. Dhuoda sees this political position as an evangelical vocation appropriate for one who must shape the world as well as endure its various temptations.

In all of these theological tasks, Dhuoda works consistently upon earlier and traditional texts which, to her, constituted an authentic—though not exhaustive—explanation of the divine mysteries. The extent to which she quotes from others and mirrors their ideas—as well as the time I have spent analyzing her use of earlier materials—may blur her own accomplishments, especially for those not familiar with medieval authors. Perhaps a word needs to be said on her behalf and in my own defense. The influence of the earlier tradition upon all medieval theology (including the great scholastics such as Aquinas) cannot be overestimated. But to assert and demonstrate that influence is to deny neither the originality nor the importance of medieval exegesis and biblical theology. Development of the exegetical tradition (as distinct from its mere repetition) can be measured by the degree to which the medieval author allowed her own lived experience of the mystery of salvation to modify, challenge and re-shape the received tradition. Certainly, the challenge or modification is not always overt. But the emphasis upon the application of the tradition to new circumstances often indicates a significant modification of meaning. Similarly, to quote or paraphrase an earlier author is not always to reiterate the thought of that author. The context of the reference to an authority, the way in which citations are juxtaposed, can reveal a subtle but meaningful critique or development.

A final caveat. My work on Dhuoda has not been significantly informed by a feminist methodology. My intent throughout has been to expose Dhuoda's writing as an example of the varied and complex biblical theology produced in the early middle ages and too often dismissed without a careful study. The absence of comparable texts by other women in the same period precludes, I believe, appropriate judgments about what might be a particularly feminine aspect to Dhuoda's theology. On the other hand, I hope that no one will miss the fact that a laywoman wrote this book and that she did so conscious of her temerity. The intensely personal quality of her theological reflection may also strike many as consonant with the character of contemporary feminist theology. If I can persuade that Dhuoda is, in fact, doing genuinely exegetical and theological work, then her place within the "lost history" of women is made more prominent. When, toward the end of the *Liber,* she prays Jacob's biblical blessing upon her son William's head, she attributes the words of blessing to both Rebeccah and Isaac, though in the text of the Vulgate they are Isaac's alone.[5] Thus she subverts, if subtly, the masculine dominance of the text by attending to the women hidden within it. Our attention to her work can broaden our understanding of early medieval biblical interpretation; let it also remind us to continue to look for those who have shaped the theological project in ways as yet unacknowledged.

---

[5] IX, 4, 23–26. Gen 28:3.

Chapter One

DHUODA IN HISTORICAL CONTEXT

The Historical Situation of the Author

Dhuoda and Her Family

Nothing is presently known with any certainty about the author of the *Liber Manualis* except what she herself tells us in the text. She was married to Bernard, son of William of Gellone, in the church at Aachen on June 30, 824. She bore him two sons: William, born in 826, and a second, born just before she began her text in 841. She cannot give us the name of the second son because she does not know it: he has been taken to his father before he could be baptized. She herself is residing at Uzès, the city whose bishop Elefantus was commissioned to bring the infant to Bernard, his father, along with William, the older son. She asserts that she is of a family equal in rank to that of her husband and there is no reason to doubt it: both her education and the cast of her mind, with its strong sense of the obligations of nobility, support her claim.

Dhuoda wrote a work that is acknowledged to be in literate, though not literary, Latin and is filled with references to the Scriptures, the Fathers and some classical authors.[6] Her text is also full of abundant praise for the value of reading as a christianizing and ennobling exercise. Here is a woman both educated and full of enthusiasm for learning. Further, she asserts that she has helped her husband in his activities in the Spanish March and other places; she has borrowed money on his behalf but presumably in her own

---

[6] Peter Dronke, *Women Writers of the Middle Ages* (London: Cambridge University Press, 1984), 36–54.

name since she feels responsible for the debts and asks her son to repay them, should any remain at her death. She is obviously an aristocratic woman who takes an active part in business affairs; she is not unique among her peers in assuming such authority.[7]

Of her husband's family much more is known.[8] Bernard was the son of Duke William of Gellone, count of Toulouse, who was himself a cousin by marriage to Charlemagne. William was a strong supporter of Louis, the king of Aquitaine, and under his authority had held universal military command against the Arabs, ruling in Narbonne in 791. In 804, he retired from active military and civil life to the monastery of Gellone, which he had founded near Aniane. His son Bernard first came to prominence in the troubles on the frontier of the Spanish March. The Count of Barcelona and Marquis Bera, having agitated treason, were replaced by Count Rampon of Gerona. The excesses of these Frankish functionaries were such that the Goths finally rose up against them and Bernard was sent to quell the uprising. He became master of the Spanish March around the year 825 or 827.[9] This was, of course, just after the time of his marriage to Dhuoda

---

[7] Book X, 4. See also Archibald Lewis, *The Development of Southern French and Catalan Society* (Austin: University of Texas Press, 1965), 170–71, and Suzanne Wemple, *Women in Frankish Society* (Philadelphia: University of Pennsylvania Press, 1984), 98–99.

[8] English translations of the contemporary chronicles make the events of Bernard's life easily accessible. Cf. *Carolingian Chronicles*, trans. by Bernhard Walter Scholtz with Barbara Rogers (Ann Arbor: University of Michigan Press, 1970); Allen Cabaniss, *Son of Charlemagne: A Contemporary Life of Louis the Pious* (Syracuse: SUNY Press, 1961). See also J. Calmette, *De Bernard, Sancti Wilelmi filio* (Toulouse, 1902); "La famille de Saint Guillem," *Annales de Midi* XVIII (1906); Joachim Wollasch, "Eine adlige Familie des frühen Mittelalters: Ihr Selbständnis und ihre Wirklichkeit," *Archiv für Kulturgeschichte* 39 (1957), 150–88.

[9] Ferdinand Lot, Christian Pfister, Francois Ganshof, *Histoire du Moyen Âge* I (Paris, 1928), 487–88.

and the year of exemption from military service arranged by Charlemagne to celebrate the marriage.[10]

The second marriage of Louis the Pious to Judith, daughter of Count Welf, the Alaman noble, bore fruit in a son born in 823. Judith had a strong sense of personal and familial rights, the rights of inheritance, which brought her into conflict with Wala, one of Louis's chief royal counsellors, whose plan was for a unified empire. Judith found a strong supporter in Bernard of Septimania and had him recalled to the court.[11] Wala attributed his support to the amorous hold the empress had over him and this was the account of his behavior given in the chronicle of Paschasius Radbertus. Nithard in his *Chronicles of the Sons of Louis the Pious* also records the tales and is generally critical of Bernard. More likely, however, it was Judith's policy of self-interest that attracted him: his son, William, whom he probably schooled in his own image, would continue to pursue a policy of family inheritance that eventually brought about his own downfall.[12]

In 830, Louis's three older sons rose up against him and his plan to redivide the empire; Bernard favored the rebellious sons and when Louis won, Bernard fled to Catalonia. He was ruling the Narbonne in 834, as his father had done before him.[13] In 835 Bernard returned to imperial favor and received Toulouse and other counties of Septimania.

---

[10] Lionel Albousse, *Histoire de la Ville d' Uzès* (Uzès, 1903), 30. Her second son was probably conceived during the year of mourning proclaimed for the death of Louis the Pious, during which time, again, the lords were given leave from military service.

[11] Lot, Pfister and Ganshof, 488–90.

[12] See Constance B. Bouchard, "Family Structure and Family Consciousness among the Aristocracy in the Ninth to Eleventh Centuries," *Francia* 14 (1986): 639–58, for the attempts to create patrilineal inheritance in the late Carolingian period.

[13] Lewis, 96, n. 135.

Louis the Pious died in 840 and the dynastic wars broke out anew. Bernard backed the fortunes of Pepin II but was eventually reconciled to Charles the Bald, during which period he offered his son William as hostage and pledge of his fidelity to Charles. In the text, Dhuoda calls Charles William's liege lord. In 844, Bernard was executed for treason. Nithard's history records it briefly: "In 844 Charles was able to lure him to the court and had him sentenced to death."[14]

After his father's death, William, for whom the *Liber* was written, continued his father's fidelity to Pepin II against Charles the Bald. In 848-9, he made a short-lived attempt to regain his territorial rights, invading Catalonia and allying himself with the Moslems. Beaten in battle, he was slain trying to secure himself in Barcelona in 850, the city awarded to his father in 826 and his father's refuge in 830.[15]

It may be that Bernard's second son, also called Bernard, was more effective in realizing his father's dynastic dream. It is difficult to track his career through the many references to persons named Bernard in the chronicles. But he is probably Bernard Plantevelue who eventually numbered among his territories the Toulousain, which had been under his grandfather's jurisdiction eighty years before.[16] If so, then he also received and passed on an inheritance of respect for monastic institutions. In 882, he gave significant gifts to the monastery of Conques and his son, Duke William the Pious, founded the great abbey of Cluny. Bernard Plantevelue died in 886.

---

[14] Scholtz, 12.

[15] Rosamond McKitterick, *The Frankish Kingdoms under the Carolingians 751-987* (New York: Longmans, 1983).

[16] Bouchard, 642, n. 10.

The City of Uzès

The history of the city in which Dhuoda wrote the *Liber Manualis* reflects the fortunes of the south of France from Roman times through the high middle ages. It always seemed to be on the border of desirable or controverted territory as well as on critical routes of communication and commerce.[17] During the height of Roman domination, it was important as a source of fresh water for the city of Nîmes; a magnificent aqueduct, built about 20 B.C., diverted the water of the Eure river from Uzès to Nîmes, some 25 miles away. Dependence upon such a water source made Nîmes vulnerable to siege and the aqueduct ceased to be maintained after the fourth century, but that awesome section of it known today as the Pont du Gard remained to keep alive the memory of Uzès's ancient importance and close ties to Nîmes, then a significant Mediterranean port.

An ancient crypt indicates the presence of a significant Christian community in Uzès from the second century.[18] Since Uzès is on the route from the Mediterranean ports to Lyon, a Christian community was probably founded there at the same time as or slightly earlier than the historic church of Lyon (c. 177). Local traditions, which survive even today in the commentary of the crypt's guide, assert that the crypt was the refuge for early Christians during imperial persecutions. The crypt of Uzès contains two rather crude bas-reliefs, an orante which seems to have been made into a christus by pounding nails into the upraised hands and a patron saint, possibly John the Baptist, incised above what seems to be a simple baptismal font. Uzès was said to have

---

[17] A. Dupont, "Uzès pendant les périodes du haut Moyen Âge, "*École Antique de Nîmes*, XXI Session (1940), 56. Cf. also C. T. Smith, *Historical Geography of Western Europe* (New York: Praeger 1967), 13, who notes that trade between Lyons and various Spanish towns perdured throughout the Muslim raids of the eight century and that Uzès was on one of the major trade routes of the period.

[18] Pierre Beraud, *Uzès, son diocèse, son histoire* (Uzès: Editions de la Cigale, 1947), 20.

a bishop from the middle of the fourth century, but no trace remains of the earliest bishops.[19]

In the beginning of the fifth century Uzès had the status of a Roman "castrum." It was an important military out-post, guarding the northeast extremity of Provence as well as the many roads which converged there.[20] In 419, Uzès received its first noteworthy bishop, Constantius, of an old Gallo-Roman family.   He participated in discussions with Pope St. Leo over the organization of the episcopal structure of Provence; he was present at the first Council of Orange (441), that of Vaison (442), and at the second and third Councils of Arles (451 and 461 respectively).   In 462 he became the metropolitan of the Narbonnaise while remaining in residence at Uzès.[21] At some point between 462 and the Council of Agde in 506, Uzès underwent occupation by the Visigoths: Probatius, the bishop of Uzès who signed the decrees of the Council of Agde, did so as a representative of that barbarian state.[22]

For the next 200 years or so, the city of Uzès was the locus of numerous struggles for control in the Midi and the south of France between the Merovingians and the kingdoms of Burgundy, Austrasia and Provence. As political control changed hands, so too episcopal authority varied and Uzès was at different times under the authority of Bourges, Aix, Marseille and Narbonne.[23] During the first century of these struggles, Uzès was fortunate in its bishops: Roricius, St-Fermin, and St-Ferreol guided the city in

---

[19] Beraud, 21.

[20] Dupont, "Uzès," 56.

[21] Beraud, 22.

[22] Beraud, 23. The decrees of the council show an interesting mixture of concern over monastic and clerical discipline, the drawing of minimal requirements of the Catholic laity in regard to fasting and Eucharistic participation and the desire to regulate the baptism of Jews.

[23] Dupont, "Uzès," 57–60. Cf. also Raoul Busquet, V–L. Bourrilly, and Maurice Agulhon, *Histoire de la Provence* (Paris, 1972), 23–28.

affairs religious and civil with marked sanctity, wisdom and intelligence. They seemed, to early historians, to maintain the ancient Roman tradition of *pietas* and literate civil service; this accounts for the tradition, discounted by contemporary historians, that all three bishops were united by family ties and descended from Tonnance Ferreol, an ancient Roman who had become prefect of the Gauls.[24] Whatever their genealogy, their cultural legacy to Uzès was to keep alive the city's roots in its classical past, the literary and legal traditions of ancient Rome. Indeed, one contemporary author asserts that Burgundian and Austrasian divisions did not seem to disturb the essential Roman unity of the region of Provence where barbarian elements, such as they were, were like nuts in the Gallo-Roman mass.[25]

As the eighth century began, a new predator appeared and Uzès was at some point taken by the Saracens in their massive invasions of 725 and 732. It is difficult to know exactly what were the conditions of this Saracen occupation because the reconquest by Charles Martel, in all respects a truly punitive series of assaults, left little evidence of the period.[26] By 754 or 756, however, Uzès was thoroughly incorporated into the Frankish Empire[27] and for just under a hundred years the city enjoyed a period of peace and growth. The Carolingians undertook the restructuring of the administration of the south and building went on apace.[28] The cathedral of St. Theodorit in Uzès was rebuilt and many smaller churches were constructed in the regions around Uzès. A donation of land given to the cathedral in 823 indicates that a community of

---

[24] Beraud, 24–31.

[25] Busquet et al, 28.

[26] *HGL*, t. I, 803–05; A. Dupont, *Quelques aspects de la vie rurale en Septimanie Carolingienne* (Montpellier, 1954), 1.

[27] *HGL*, 825; Dupont, "Uzès," 65.

[28] Dupont, "La vie rurale," 2-3.

canons had been set up by that period, enhancing the dignity of both town and cathedral. The same donation indicates that Uzès had become an imperial "comte," a jurisdictional unit set up to foster colonization and the development of productive land.[29]

Uzès was a beneficiary of Carolingian policy which sought to provide sufficient security for a true renaissance of rural life and activity. Charles' policies effectively incorporated the church into the pursuit of security and development; he sought to inspire bishops to renew their dioceses spiritually and temporally. But he placed his greatest hopes in a strong network of monasteries which were to be built in the tradition of Benedict of Aniane and which would provide not only for the productivity of the land but also for the cultural development of the people through education and the copying of manuscripts.[30] The bishops of Uzès exemplify the implementation of Carolingian policy, especially Sigibert, who became bishop around 768 and Arimond, his successor. Sigibert was a Frank who, in addition to writing a history of the kings of the Franks, tried to improve the quality of the clergy through examinations and encouraged the building of schools in all his churches. Arimond, who attended the Council of Narbonne to attend to the question of adoptionism, oversaw the founding of numerous Benedictine monasteries in which manuscripts and outbuildings alike gave witness to the reclamation of the riches of the past—its literature and its arable land.[31]

In its building of churches and monasteries, its land development and imperial administration, Uzès was like most other cities in the Rhone Valley, that rich border area between Provence and Languedoc. But Uzès could also boast of the presence of an episcopal mint. The minting of gold coins was such

---

[29] Dupont, "Uzès," 65–66; Cf. also Busquet et al, 29 and Dupont, "La vie rurale," 7.

[30] Dupont, "La vie rurale," 5–6; Beraud, 45.

[31] Beraud, 42–43.

a rarity in the Carolingian empire that many historians have felt called upon to comment on the presence of the mint at Uzès, which had been active from the time of the Merovingians and would continue to be licensed into the middle of the twelfth century. Some see the antiquity of its privilege as the reason why Uzès alone was allowed to operate its mint during Carolingian times. Others believe that it was permitted in order to induce Spanish Jews to trade with Uzès, long a commercial center of some importance. It has also been suggested that the mint served only to provide some very few coins to be used not for exchange but as gift medallions. Whatever the reasons for its existence, there is no doubt that it enhanced the status of the city of Uzès and added to its economic security and vitality.[32]

This peaceful state of affairs came to an end, in effect, for Uzès in 843 with the Treaty of Verdun. After that, Uzès and the rest of Provence and Languedoc again became the battlefield of dynastic controversy. The roughly ninety years of pacification and rebuilding thus ended in the very year in which Dhuoda's *Liber Manualis* was completed. This book, which she intended as a mirror for the personal growth and edification of her son, is also a mirror of the time and place which saw its achievement.[33]

Above all, perhaps, the *Liber* reflects the accomplishment of Charlemagne's dream of educational reforms and intellectual growth. Dhuoda's book is not only the product of a fairly high level of education; it also breathes forth optimism about the power of reading and learning to elevate the hearts and minds of the nobility. That the learning which Dhuoda prizes is an attempt to reclaim the classical wisdom of the ancient Christian past is further reflective of the Carolingian ideal and of the tradition of the bishops of Uzès. Whatever her genealogy, her cultural ancestry is in Roman Provence. She is kin to the sixth-century bishops with their reputation for preserving the Gallo-Roman heritage.

---

[32] Dupont, "Uzès," 67–68.

[33] Dupont, 69.

Even in small details, Dhuoda reflects her city: in the homely metaphor of the goldsmiths at work, Dhuoda reveals first-hand observation; it does not take much imagination to see her watching the artisans in the mint at Uzès. She also mentions having borrowed money from both Jews and Christians. There are some indications that the situation of the Jews in southern France was one of factual tolerance and civic involvement. In 449, for instance, the Jewish community at Arles took part in the obsequies of the Bishop St. Hilary, chanting psalms in Hebrew as they accompanied the bier in the funeral procession. They participated in a similar way in the entombment of Bishop Caesarius in 543 and this must have been sufficiently general a custom to provoke the Council of Narbonne (589) to formulate canon 9, which forbade Jews to celebrate funeral processions with the singing of psalms.[34] However, as late as the seventh century, a prominent Jew in Narbonne inscribed an epitaph to his three dead children using Hebrew characters. Such a public display of the Jewish religion argues a certain uncommon tolerance on the part of the bishops of the Narbonnaise.[35] This kind of tolerance seems to have marked the hierarchical church at Uzès as well. In 558, Bishop St-Ferreol experienced a kind of exile imposed on him by Childebert, the King of the Franks, for having friendly intercourse with the Jewish community of that city. Apparently he had violated official policy by inviting them to share the hospitality of his table.[36]

A visitor today can see in Uzès, and in other towns and cities of the region, the continual process of rebuilding at one key moment of which Dhuoda wrote her *Liber Manualis*. Dressed stones from every period are used again and again as buildings are rebuilt, restored and enlarged. Roman pediments and pillars find

---

[34] Dupuy, 45. Cf. Mansi, IX, c. 1016.

[35] Michel Chalon, "L'inscription juive de Narbonne et la condition des Juifs en Narbonnaise à la fin du VIIe siecle," *Homage à Andrè Dupont* (Montpellier, 1974), 51.

[36] Beraud, 28–29; Dupont, 63.

their way into tenth-century chapels and twelfth-century naves.[37] With the eminent practical realism of those whose homes were on the crossroads of continual warfare, the citizens of Uzès regularly utilized what was left of the past to construct edifices with new functions that reflected a new spirit. In a similar way, Dhuoda mines the past—both classical and Christian—for the perennial wisdom which she will re-organize to serve a new function. She thus achieves a thoroughly traditional Christian theology that has been reshaped to serve the needs of the emerging feudal world. In its spirit and structure, Dhuoda's *Liber Manualis* reflects the method and creative energy of the citizens of her city of Uzès. Her book, like their stones, carries the rich heritage of the past across a tenuous present into an emerging future.

The Literary Situation of Dhuoda

The Author's Persona
    Though Dhuoda intends this *Liber Manualis* for the education of her son, it is filled with her self-revelations. The image she projects of herself is complex. Certainly, a strong thread of self-disclaiming affirmations runs through the whole. While these may often be no more than the conventional *topos* of humility adopted by medieval authors, a closer examination of Dhuoda's text reveals that she often gives them a personal dimension. Above all, she is filled with a sense of the transience of all human activity (part of the medieval *topos,* to be sure) but especially of the waning historical importance of her own family. She is also genuinely aware of her own limitations as scholar and theologian. At the same time, Dhuoda attributes to herself significant public roles, doing so with an emphasis and a tone of self-justification that indicate her sense of her own temerity.

---

[37] The church at Vaison-les-Romains is the most striking example, with its massive white Roman pillar in the nave and classical pedestals particularly visible from the outside.

At first glance, a reader might assume that her self-disclaiming statements reflect her feelings of inferiority as a woman. A closer reading reveals, however, that she consistently identifies her "unworthiness" with her *humanity*, not her femininity. In the epigrams contained in the prefatory material, she says that she is unworthy because she is "frail, in exile, turning into dust."[38] In the first chapter she tells us directly, "Certainly I know better than anyone else the condition of my human frailty; I reproach myself unceasingly for I am but poor dust and ashes" (I, i). Dust and ashes signify her status as creature, her inevitable journey into death, even her sinfulness, but it says nothing about her as a woman. She underlines this thought a few lines later when she says that she is "insignificant and of lowly birth," by which she probably means, as she says elsewhere, that her family is of slight importance because their fortunes are in decline (IV, iii). The sense of the evanescence of all human things is not just a kind of Platonic *Weltanschauung* for Dhuoda. Rather, her sense of the world as passing is historical and social. In the Carolingian world that itself faces decline through civil war, she is literally both weak and insignificant because her family (her birth family, not that into which she has married) has been on the downside of historical forces and no longer has either power or authority.[39] She explicitly attributes her lack of merit to the historical shifts of fortune to which she and her family may have been subject (X, iv). Her family's history has thus reinforced the traditional *topos* and has given specific content to the more general religious conviction: all transient things are

---

[38] "Certe et ego ipsa, considerans casum humanae fragilitatis meae, me reprehendi indesimenter non cesso, cum sim misera, cinisque et puluis" (I ,1, 14–17).

[39] She says, in Book I, 4, that her own relatives, as also William's, have lost power and died. Bouchard considers the possibility that Dhuoda mentions two of her own family members in the list of those to be prayed for (Book X, 5). If so, one of those mentioned, Guarnarius, may have been murdered in 814 after attempting to reform the court of Louis the Pious (642, n. 14).

inferior to God and God's kingdom that will last forever (Cf. I, ix; III, i).

At the same time, other statements indicate that she does not appraise her own gifts highly. In the preface she tells William that her book will be small, "as is the measure of her understanding." From then on, she almost always calls it "this small book." When she describes the book she points out that it is not an organized treatise, neither is it original. It is a collection and it is imitative (I, v). In the middle ages, however, these "flaws" would be considered virtues. The most talented scholars would continue to denigrate their own work in relation to the Fathers of the church and the ancient philosophers. The medieval mind saw intentional originality as a betrayal of the tradition and imitation as the closest possible approximation of the genius of the "golden age" to which they continually harked back. So Dhuoda is saying neither more nor less about her work than writers and scholars would say for several more centuries to come. At the same time, she begins a written work for which there is no known precedent. Though the genre of the *mirror* was well known and used in her environment, there was no literary tradition of written handbooks from parents to children, much less from mothers to sons, and Dhuoda's innovation here must be acknowledged.

For the rest, she simply states that she has her faults and enumerates some of them, surely an obvious thing for a mother to explain to her son whom she is trying to lead to spiritual growth. She acknowledges that she is lukewarm and lazy in prayer, weak and inclined to "inferior things," by which Dhuoda means any human or earthly reality (II, v). She affirms that her teaching about God does not come from mystical experience (I, i); she has had to work hard for her understanding of divine things, undoubtedly through study and the thoughtful experience of life, particularly its "tribulations." She sees that her wisdom has come from God through these ordinary channels and she is duly grateful (Pref; Epigrams; I, ii). Parallels for these statements can be found in any medieval religious text.

What one is not likely to find, even in much later texts, is Dhuoda's calm assumption of significant public roles, roles which were definitively closed to women by custom and even by law.[40] With increasing confidence throughout the *Liber Manualis*, Dhuoda appropriates to herself the public roles of writer, counsellor and teacher, all of which would have been considered outside her competence as a woman.

She acknowledges herself as a writer from the very beginning of her work. Toward the end of Chapter One, she tells us how she understands and evaluates the writer's gift and task. She says that ". . . if all the people born into all the cultures of the world were to be made writers by a sudden increase of human genius . . ."[41] still they would be unable to capture in words the grandeur of God (I, 6, 6–8). So writing is not an ordinary gift; and throughout the work she refers to herself as a conscious, crafting writer. She acknowledges the difficulties, telling us in the preface that she has struggled to make the book a good work (Inc. 45–52). In the same passage, she indicates that she knows what elements go into good writing: the relationship between structure and meaning, the scanning which creates poetry and a certain "fluidity" which makes for good prose (38–40). Elsewhere she acknowledges that writing requires "sharpness of mind" and calls it a "perilous public contest" (I, 1, 12–14), language that links her task to tournaments and public debates with all their exigencies and consequences.

---

[40] Concerning the impact of earlier Christian theory on Frankish women, see Suzanne Fonay Wemple, *Women in Frankish Society* (Philadelphia: University of Pennsylvania Press, 1981), 9–25. For the earlier theory and legislation, see also Roger Gryson, *The Ministry of Women in the Early Church*, translated by Jean LaPorte and Mary Louise Hall (Collegeville, Minn.: Liturgical Press, 1980); Elizabeth A. Clark, *Women in the Early Church* (Wilmington, Delaware: Glazier,1983); Barbara J. MacHaffie, *Her Story: Women in Christian Tradition* (Philadelphia: Fortress Press, 1986), 28–29. On Dhuoda's self-imaging, see Dronke, 41–43.

[41] "Atque ipsi orbi cultures cuncti, nascentes in mundum, ob ingenio humanitatis augmentum omnes fuissent Scriptores. . ."(I, 6, 6–8).

The word "public" is a critical one. Dhuoda is not writing this book only for William, though he is its primary audience; she envisions a wider public. At the end of the prefatory epigrams, she writes:

> Reader, you who desire to know the plan,
> Follow the appropriate beginnings of these verses.
> Then you will be able to understand with quick steps,
> The meaning which I have written below.
> The mother of two sons,. . .[42]

Obviously, she expects the reader to be other than those children of whom she speaks in the third person. Additionally, she says at the beginning of Chapter one that she feels herself in the presence of those to whom William will offer the book for reading (I, 1, 9–11). Finally she speaks again to the wider audience in the framing of her epitaph: "And if someone [else] reads this manual which you now read, let him meditate on the words that follow."[43] Dhuoda gives evidence of her self-consciousness as a writer from the beginning to the end of the *Liber Manualis*.

The role of counsellor, on the other hand, she consciously assumes in only one place. At the heart of Book III on William's secular vocation is an exposition of the role of counsellors; Dhuoda gives William advice both on being a counsellor and on choosing counsellors for himself. In the midst of this advice, she introduces herself as one of his counsellors:

---

[42] "Lector qui cupis formulam nosse, capita perquire abta uersorum. Exin ualebis concito gradu sensu cognosci quae sim conscripta. Genitrix duorum masculini sexus," Epig, 80–87.

[43] "Sed et istum Manualem quem legis, qui legerit umquam, uerba quae subtus secuntur meditetur ipse. . ." (X 6, 10–12).

There are some who consider themselves counsellors and they are not; they judge themselves to be wise when they are not. "If I say less, I am more so."[44]

The quotation from Paul's justification of his apostleship underlines Dhuoda's assertion: she is to be considered among those—few in number in those difficult days—who are "worthy and useful and truthful" in the most difficult of public, indeed political, roles, the advising of the powerful.

Both as counsellor and writer, Dhuoda has been drawn into her public roles because of the unusual circumstances in which she must exercise her more customary role of mother. This maternal role also causes her to assume the role of teacher, a role she takes even greater pains to document and which would have been closed to her not only by custom but more particularly by ecclesiastical law. Basing their restrictions on an interpretation of 1 Tim 2:12, church authorities had consistently enacted legislation which prevented women from entering into the teaching of church doctrine, even in the earlier centuries when certain sacramental roles were still open to women. According to the traditional interpretation it was Paul himself (though the attribution is no longer universally accepted) who proclaimed: "I do not permit a woman to act as teacher or in any way to have authority over a man; she must be quiet." Against this text, understood as apostolic and reinforced by centuries of ecclesiastical legislation, Dhuoda's projection of herself as a valid, indeed irreplaceable, religious teacher to her sons is remarkable.

Dhuoda clearly sees her teaching role as an extension of her maternal one. This forms the basis of her self-justification. In the Prologue, she acknowledges that her attempt to teach religious doctrine to William demands justification (it is, by the way, the only place where she refers to herself as a member of the "weaker

---

[44] "Sunt nonnulli qui quasi consiliarii se arbitrantur esse, et non sunt, existimantes se sapientes cum non sint ita. `Si minus dicam, plus ego'" (III, 6, 1–3).

sex"). But she goes on to offer William her manual of instruction with the simple explanation that, after all, she is his mother. She offers it diffidently at first, however, comparing her book to a board game, to which others like him have daily recourse from the tedium of every-day tasks. She has thus minimized her action to that of a mother offering entertainment to her child.

Later she becomes bolder, asserting that her role is to lead William to a deeper understanding of God, in spite of her unworthiness (I, 4, 12–14). Indeed, she soon dares to affirm that she will be his best teacher, best in the sense that her teaching will have special power in his life because her "burning heart" imparts to her words a unique character (I, 7, 20–23). She becomes even bolder, affirming that all Christian mothers are inherently teachers; she seeks precedent for this assertion in antiquity and in tradition. In the discussion (Book VII) of the two births, physical and spiritual, that every human being must undergo, she puts forth the simple principle that the one who is most active in the first birth ought to be similarly concerned and active in the second. She cites several mothers who have been honored by the church for having brought about the baptismal second birth in the lives of their children and concludes with the sweeping statement that Christian women have been teachers and spiritual guides to their children in all generations.

> Then, now, and always, many women unceasingly give daily birth to their sons in holy church "through the gospel" as it is said, by the preaching of sacred doctrine or by the example of frequent good works.[45]

Not only is the role of teacher appropriate for mothers, not only does their affection give special power to their words, but Dhuoda also believes that a mother has special pedagogical skill to suit the

---

[45] "Et multi tunc et nunc et semper, *per Euangelium*, inquid, et doctrinam sanctae praedicationis, uel exemplum conuersationis operum bonorum, cotidie in sancta Ecclesia non desinunt generare filios" (VII, 3, 15–19).

teaching to the capacity of the learner, knowing as she does the slow stages through which a child develops. Christian tradition had suggested as much by consistently comparing religious education to spiritual nourishment. Paul himself had spoken in maternal imagery of his own teaching of the Corinthians, saying that he gave them milk rather than solid food (1 Cor 3:2). Dhuoda applies his words to herself, showing how she has broken down the sublime teaching about the beatitudes and the gifts of the Holy Spirit into modest teaching that he can grasp a little at a time, beginning with milk and progressing to solid food until he is ready for heavenly food (VI, 1, 14–18).

So confident has Dhuoda become as she works out the justification for her teaching role that we are not surprised to find her departing from the literal and accepted meaning of a particular text and teaching William her own interpretation of it. This departure occurs in the context of her teaching on the first and second birth, the precise section in which she seems most conscious of her own power as a teacher. She is attempting to show William that his "carnal" or physical reality and his spiritual self are completely mutual and interactive components of his total personal reality. Again, she quotes Paul in support of her idea. She misquotes him, in fact, as Riché points out,[46] reminding us that a misquotation for one is often another's "interpretation." Then she says with great authority: "Though this passage actually means something else, for various good reasons, I want you to understand it here in the way I reveal."[47]

It seems evident that Dhuoda is aware that taking on the role of teacher exposes her to censure. She takes pains to connect this function with the role which both society and church assigned and would accept. In the course of writing her manual, she seems to grow in confidence, moving from a desire to show that her teaching

---

[46] p. 299, n. 3.

[47] "Et licet aliter hoc in loco uoluatur sensus, pro certis differentium causis, ego uolo ut ita teneas sicut fateor" (VII, 1, 16–18).

is not harmful to William (it is an innocent diversion such as a board game) to a conviction that as a mother her teaching will have a special power for him. It will move him on an emotional level because of her burning heart and it will be more appropriate to his developing mind because she understands the stages of that development and can tailor her teaching to it. Finally she arrives at a confidence that enables her to teach on her own authority, to change the meaning of a text because it is more appropriate to what she is teaching. Like many another, Dhuoda has become a teacher by teaching.

The Text in its Literary Context

Dhuoda calls her book a *handbook*; she further describes it as a mirror in which William can study the state of his own soul (Pro 21–22) and several scholars have shown the way in which her text fits into the tradition of the *speculum* so popular in her day.[48] Bessmertny describes the general characteristics of the Carolingian *speculum* according to a scheme organized by P. Toubert. These characteristics are four: 1) the mirror is ordinarily a very free composition, structured only by an obligatory comparison between the virtues and the vices; 2) central to the mirror is a social ideal formed from the marriage of Christian morality with the moral code of the warrior; 3) significant dependence on Augustinian thought controls the development of its argumentation; and 4) content of the mirror is largely determined by the reader for whom it is intended. Seen against these general characteristics, Dhuoda's *Handbook* does indeed appear to be a true Carolingian *speculum*. But because hers is so personal a text, it is much more than this: it has the air of a spiritual last will and testament with elements of a primitive catechism. It is also something of a genealogical work, listing the names and relationships of the ancestors for whom William is

---

[48] See in particular Y. Bessmertny, "Le monde vu par une femme noble au IXe siècle: La perception du monde dans l'aristocratie carolingienne," *Moyen Âge* 93 (1987): 162–84. Also, Ritamary Bradley, "Backgrounds of the Title *Speculum* in Medieval Literature," *Speculum* 29 (1954): 100–15.

bound to pray. Finally, it is a modest attempt at a kind of educational primer with rudimentary introductions into the required learning of the day, such as grammar, etymologies and computation. It is a mirror, then, not only in the sense usually understood by that literary form, but a mirror of the personal world of Dhuoda, circumscribed and yet redolent of the larger world of political and social change. Indeed, Dhuoda herself calls it a mirror of her own soul, even her own personality. "As you read this book with your body and with your mind," she tells William, "you will be able to see me as a picture in the mirror."[49] In Dhuoda's hands, the Carolingian mirror reflects a wide variety of images: the ideal knight, the concrete dangers and opportunities in the political world, and, not least of all, the concerns, character and interior life of Dhuoda herself. Her *Liber* is not completely understood if seen only as an example of the Carolingian *speculum*. It needs the wider context of Carolingian scholarship as its frame.

It is easy enough to affirm, as I have above, that Dhuoda was formed by the Carolingian reforms in education. Certainly, an emphasis on the importance of books and learning runs through her work as a dominant thread. For her, learning is a necessary part of spiritual growth. Indeed she says emphatically, "There are no riches where stupidity reigns and, in contrast, no hindrance where gracious speech is carefully exercised.[50] Note that the contrast is between "stupidity" and "gracious speech." It is abundantly clear that what she means by learning is the education to be found in books, learning which begins with an emphasis upon the correct use of language. On every page she quotes her sources or paraphrases them, thus insistently reminding William of the authors where wisdom is to be found. Numerous injunctions to read occur throughout the work; over and over again Dhuoda tells William to

---

[49] "Quasi in picturam speculi, me mente et corpore legendo et Deum deprecando intueri possis. . ."(I, 7, 17–19).

[50] "Non sunt diuitiae uni regnat stultitia, et nichil deest obstans in rebus ubi assiduus militatur sermo eucarus" (III, 5, 26–27).

read the book she sends, read the Fathers, read *Pastoral Care* by Gregory the Great, read *The Synonyms* of Isidore of Seville. She assumes in the Prologue that he owns books and will continue to acquire them; she is anxious that her own modest volume be not lost among the many he will come to own. She encourages him to acquire more books and to beg for learning. She is obviously imbued with the understanding that guided the educational reforms of Carolingian rulers: the written word contains the power to elevate the spirit and moral development is dependent upon intellectual development. For this reason, one of the areas of scholarship that has most utilized the evidence of Dhuoda's *Liber* is the study of scholarship and literacy in the Carolingian age.

It is important, however, to be more specific about the kind of Carolingian intellectual and textual activity against which Dhuoda's work can be most properly appraised.[51] Recent scholarship has done much to expose the general literacy of the Carolingian aristocracy. Rosamund McKitterick, among others, has compiled a persuasive body of evidence. Most recently she argues "that in the prodigious output of the written word at every level of Carolingian society we are observing the essential phases in the development of a literate culture, with new ideals and definitions of education and knowledge dependent on a written tradition."[52] She analyzes the evidence for this "prodigious output" in the increased use of writing in the legal processes of the empire; she evaluates the economic dimension of books, indicators of what Carolingians

---

[51] See John J. Contreni, "Education in the Carolingian World," *Annals of Scholarship* 1 (1980): 81–96, for a brief look at the many different ways scholars have interpreted the so-called Carolingian "renaissance." Contreni holds the view that "the immediate effect of their [political and religious leaders] involvement in learning and culture was to stimulate activity on a broad front. Over distances of time and space, however, the original impetus was transformed through the prism of individual talent and local differences," 83. Dhuoda's work exemplifies Contreni's statement.

[52] *The Carolingians and the Written Word.* (New York and Cambridge: Cambridge University Press, 1989), 3.

were prepared to spend their money on and what they believed to enhance their social status. From library catalogs and book inventories, she draws the principles by which Carolingians organized their knowledge and the perimeters within which they exercised their literary and intellectual accomplishments. She moves, finally, to a careful analysis of both the possibilities and the actualities of lay literacy and the influence of this literacy on Carolingian religious sensibility. In her discussion of the evidence offered by the text of the *Liber Manualis* she asks whether Dhuoda is to be considered "a rare instance of a Carolingian bluestocking" or whether we might be justified in seeing her as representative. "Fragments of other evidence extant, in the form of works dedicated to or commissioned by laywomen, books owned by them, borrowed or given to them, indeed, make an assessment of Dhuoda as one well-documented instance of a general phenomenon more than mere wishful thinking."[53] The extended commitment of Pierre Riché, the editor of the *Liber Manualis* for *SC*, to the study of lay education in the early medieval period is documented in McKitterick's voluminous notes. In his introduction to the *Liber*, he summarizes Dhuoda's use of her sources. He notes her fondness for the grammarians and the glossaries of the time, her acquaintance with the theories of digital computation and her direct dependence on Prudence, the Merovingian poets, and the Fathers of the church, in particular Augustine and Gregory the Great. Among later authors, she makes use of Isidore of Seville and certain of her contemporaries: Ambrose Autpert, Alcuin and Rhaban Maurus. She knows the Rule of Benedict and several passions of the martyrs.[54]

---

[53] 225.

[54] See also Richè's work in "Les Bibliothèques de trois aristocrates laïcs carolingiens," *Le Moyen Âge* 69 (1963): 87–104 and in *L'Hagiographie, cultures and sociétés* (Paris, 1981).

The question remains, of course, to what degree Dhuoda knew all of these works directly and which she knew through collections such as the florilegia and the homiliaries which began to proliferate in her own day. But the work of McKitterick and Riché leaves no doubt of the possibility that a lay aristocrat like herself could have a library comprising all the books from which Dhuoda quotes, a varied range of florilegia[55] and many other books besides. Further, McKitterick has culled wills, charters and library catalogues to document the customary *borrowing* of books from monasteries and large churches by lay aristocrats.[56]

The specific evidence of what was available in one monastery, albeit it a large and significant one, may give some indication of what was available to an aristocratic reader. According to McKitterick, a major monastic library such as that of Lorsch would have a collection of church Fathers that included Athanasius, Hilary of Poitiers, Gregory Nazianzus, Basil, Origen, Augustine, Ambrose, Chrysostom and Jerome and, among the later writers, Julian of Toledo, Isidore, Gregory the Great, Alcuin and Bede (both the historical and exegetical works).[57] Even a smaller monastery such as Murbach in the diocese of Metz had a significant body of holdings. The catalog compiled there in the mid-ninth century, which omits all biblical and liturgical books, groups the contents of its library under various headings, one of which is by author; McKitterick gives the list as follows: Cyprian, Hilary of Poitiers, Ambrose, Jerome, Augustine, Origen, Basil, John Chrysostom, Gregory I, Isidore of Seville, Bede, Cassiodorus, Cassian, Prosper, Primasius, Julian of Toledo and Gregory Nazianzus. These authors make up the library's scriptural and theological collection; other works are listed according to topics, such as history, classical prose

---

[55] For a discussion of the particular importance of florilegia in the Carolingian church and the increased production of both those and the homiliaries, see McKitterick, *Written Word*, 155–83.

[56] 261–66.

[57] *Written Word*, 185–90.

and poetry, medical books, etc. Lists such as these of works which could be borrowed by any of the aristocratic laity who did not yet possess them indicate that Dhuoda would have had the means to consult the traditional interpretations honored and zealously preserved during her time. Her *Liber*, eclectic, traditional and at the same time thoroughly personalized, is intimately connected to the kind of intellectual and literary activity which, according to Riché and McKitterick, marked the Carolingian aristocracy.

Among the many texts produced, read, borrowed and valued in the Carolingian period, the homiliary holds an important place. In his study of the homiliary books of the Carolingian school of Auxerre, Henri Barre has laid out the characteristics of this particular sub-genre that both he and McKitterick find central to Carolingian literary and ecclesiastical developments. The homiliary is, according to Barre, a collection of homiletic commentaries designed, not for liturgical reading, but for the spiritual and doctrinal enrichment of those whose lives involve them in a regular observance of the liturgical rites, principally monks and clerics. But they were also books which the laity quickly came to value. The genre seems to have its roots in the fifth century,[58] though we know these early attempts only through later works in which they were generally redacted according to the local system of readings. The late redactions are represented, *inter alia,* by the Homiliary of Agimond, a Roman priest for the church of Sts. Philip and James (c. 750) and that of Alain de Farfa (c. 770).[59]

The particular connection of the homiliary with the Carolingian period begins with Charlemagne's request that Paul the Deacon choose from the catholic fathers an appropriate selection to explain the liturgical readings for each day of the liturgical cycle. The difficulties attendant on such a task are obvious: the lack of a

---

[58] *Les homéliares Carolingiens de l'école d' Auxerre* (Vatican City: Biblioteca Apostolica Vaticana, 1962), 2.

[59] See also Reginald Grégoire, *Les Homéliaires du moyen âge, Rerum Ecclesiasticum Documenta,* Series Maior, Fontes VI (Rome: Herder, 1966).

uniform lectionary, the tendency of the fathers to compose homilies almost exclusively on the Gospels and the arduous labors, made even more onerous by the paucity of texts, of combing the patristic commentaries and tracts for appropriate selections to be included in such a homiliary. Despite all of this, the task seems to have been undertaken with vigor and enthusiasm. Barre comments that since no particular model was rigidly in place for these homiliaries, the inspiration of each compiler was given free rein. He notes several hundred examples of Carolingian provenance preserved in the libraries.[60]

The development of these Carolingian homiliaries is helpful to someone assessing Dhuoda's exegetical work. The particular characteristics by which Barre identifies homiliaries as "Carolingian" bear a striking resemblance to her exegetical work in the *Liber*, thereby situating the latter firmly within the stream of intellectual and religious activity of her own time. Of course, she is writing in an entirely different genre and there is no question of using the framework of liturgical readings. But like the authors of the various homiliaries, she is writing to open up the wisdom of the fathers to one who is in the beginning stages of religious instruction; she says so explicitly in several places. Her emphasis is primarily on the moral life of her son; she makes explicit the ways in which virtue is to be acquired and vices overcome as did many homilists, following Rhabanus. She has designed her work for private, meditative reading. And her work shares the character of an "exegetical chain;" both in her use of Scripture and her citations from the earlier works in the tradition, she weaves her borrowings together for her own purposes and with an originality that Barre and McKitterick find with increasing frequency in the homiliaries of the ninth century. When she describes her own work in Book I, Chap. 4, she says, "I cannot offer you a treatise perfectly worked out—I am not capable of that even if it were appropriate for me to do it. Rather I will try to imitate such a work by putting

---

[60] Barre, 5.

together the most helpful ideas" (14–16). Among a variety of models which she seems to have in mind, the Carolingian homiliary could have been a helpful example to her.

The Text and Its Transmission

There are three extant Latin manuscripts of the *Liber Manualis*. The oldest, the N manuscript, is at the Bibliothèque Municipale in the city of Nîmes where it is catalogued as #393. It is a sadly incomplete but beautiful tenth-century vellum manuscript containing nine fragments in 32 folios, written in Carolingian minuscule. Its early history is unknown; it was found posthumously among the papers of E. Germer-Durand, a scholar whose interest in the regional history of Nîmes led to the discovery of significant archeological remains of the Carolingian period.

The P manuscript is a seventeenth-century copy—#12.293 fonds latin—at the Bibliothèque Nationale in Paris. Mabillon in his *Acta Sanctorum Ordinis sancti Benedicti* attests that this was copied at the monastery of St. Germain-des-Près from a manuscript belonging to the library of Peter Marca, archbishop of Toulouse, later of Paris. Riché hypothesizes that Marca could have come upon the *Liber Manualis* during a seven-year stay in the city of Barcelona.[61]

The third manuscript, designated "B," is the most recently discovered; it was first brought to public notice in 1950 by A. Cordoliani. It is #569 in the Biblioteca Central de Barcelone and is of Catalan origin. Riché believes it to have been revised from an older manuscript which could have itself derived from the copy received by William, the original recipient of the book who died near Barcelona in 850.

Discovery of the N and B manuscripts led, in each case, to the publication of different Latin editions. In 1887, E. Bondurand, archivist of Gard, published a Latin edition based on a comparison

---

[61] Riché, "Introduction," 56.

of the P and N manuscripts under the title *L'Education carolingienne. Le Manuel de Dhuoda (843)*. The publication also contained a French translation that is, however, often little more than a paraphrastic summary. Incidently, the 1887 publication apparently caused quite a ripple of civic pride: the mayor of Nîmes renamed one of its streets the rue Dhuoda, for which honor M. Bondurand duly sent the mayor a note of thanks.[62]

In 1975, a new critical edition was published by SC based on the discovery of B and a comparison of the three extant manuscripts. Vol 225 of the series, the new publication, entitled *Manuel pour mon fils*, was edited by Pierre Riché and contains a French translation by Bernard de Vregille and Claude Mondesert, S.J. It was Riché who divided Dhuoda's text into eleven sections which he calls "books." This is the edition on which I have based my own study and it is the one cited in my text, following Riché's division of books and chapters. Except where noted, the translations are my own.

Working almost simultaneously with the French editors, Myra E. Bowers prepared her own edition of the Latin text based on the three manuscripts as her doctoral dissertation at Catholic University of America. This contains an English translation and introduction and was published by University Microfilms International in 1977 with the title *The Liber Manualis of Dhuoda: Advice of a Ninth-Century Mother for her Son*.

Though bits and pieces of Dhuoda's text have been translated in several anthologies, a new publication (1991) has made the entire text easily available to the English speaking world. Carol Neel's very readable translation, based on the Riché edition, has been published by the University of Nebraska Press under the title *Handbook for William: A Carolingian Woman's Counsel for Her Son*.

---

[62] This letter was shown to the author by Monsieur G. Dupré of the École de Nîmes.

Chapter Two

DHUODA IN THEOLOGICAL CONTEXT

In order to position Dhuoda as a theologian of the middle ninth century, we must first look at the general characteristics of Carolingian theology, considering what were the theological tasks undertaken and the methodologies by which those tasks were pursued. General church histories, especially those done in the first half of this century, have spoken of iconoclasm and Spanish adoptionism as the theological issues which engrossed Charlemagne and his theologians in the early decades of the period and for which the *Libri carolini* are analyzed as the result of his efforts toward orthodoxy. The middle of the ninth century is looked at through the lenses of the eucharistic controversy and the debate over predestination; in these debates, the work of Paschasius Radbertus, Rhaban Maur, Gottshalk, Ratramnus of Corbie, Hincmar and John Scotus forms the center of interest and discussion. But the theology of the ninth century was not driven exclusively by doctrinal controversy and to look only at the literature of controversy is to have too narrow a view of the theological achievements of the Carolingian period. The general renewal of church and state undertaken by Charlemagne and continued, with significant modification, by Charles the Bald spawned a good deal of constructive theology. Like the Fathers of the first four centuries (whom they resemble more than is sometimes acknowledged), ninth century theologians were concerned to develop the coherent body of doctrine which they inherited into a living reality accessible to all the people as the foundation of a faithful Christian community. It is in its pastoral and ethical dimensions that we find the framework and the living soul of Carolingian theology.

It is within this pastoral context that the work of Dhuoda is to be located; the *Liber Manualis* is, on the one hand, more than a personal spirituality for her or for her son and, on the other, less than a complete doctrinal treatise on any one topic. Indeed, Dhuoda is engaged in practical theology, more focused on the ethical issues that confront her son and his peers than on many of the doctrinal issues engaged by the better-known theologians. To be sure, for her as for her theological ancestors in the classical period, morality and the demands of Christian life were not to be understood apart from the great doctrines that made up the *depositum fidei*. Dhuoda indicates toward the end of her volume that everything that she has written has been "for [William's] salvation,"[63] a reminder that she, like the great theologians of the first four centuries, shaped her theology to a soteriological purpose. Her explanation of what she has attempted to do for William reads like a good description of biblical theology. Her goal has been to enable William to "order [his] earthly experience so that [he] may act calmly and confidently"[64] whether in his military vocation or in the contemplative life. Good theology, a living interpretation of the divine revelation, makes comprehensible one's own particular life and enables one to choose and to act with prudence and, even more, with *discretio* ("calmly and confidently"); it is the necessary precondition for every state in Christian life. Dhuoda and her contemporaries inhabited a theological world in which there was not yet a rigid separation between what would become systematic and pastoral theology. Every aspect of theology was grounded in a reading of the biblical texts; both systematic and pastoral theology were arrived at by the same kind of exegesis, at once traditional and framed by actual, contemporary questions. Within this fluid understanding, Dhuoda's emphasis, like that of many of her

---

[63] "Ex primo namque huius uersu libelli, Vsque ad ultimam eiusdem sillabam, Cuncta tibi ad pensum salutis scripta cognosce" (X, 1, 18–20).

[64] "Qualitas temporalium ut . . . secure et quiete ualeas incedere, prout ualui ordinatrix tibi astiti in cunctis" (VII, 1, 2–5). I have used Neel's translation here.

contemporaries,[65] was on the questions of social morality and a theology of the active life of the aristocratic class. To these questions she applied a variety of exegetical methods, re-working traditional interpretations to resolve new tensions, new issues and new challenges.

Homiliaries, letters covering a range of theological and pastoral issues, treatises on various aspects of imperial authority, lives of saints, liturgical treatises—the very breadth of literature produced by theologians of the ninth century testifies to the complexity of their theological program. One major concern of Carolingian theologians was the need to transmit and re-vivify the hermeneutical tradition of the classical period and the early monastic masters. This was a necessary element in the comprehensive educational dimension of imperial policy—which was not merely designed to produce manuscripts, however grateful later generations might be for that achievement. Charlemagne's final goal, at least as it was interpreted by bishop, abbot and monk, was not merely linguistic literacy but the capacity to read biblical and liturgical texts with understanding and spiritual profit, which meant the capacity to implement them within the particular circumstances of one's life. Exegesis, as understood by the early church and the monastic world, was intrinsic to this educational project and was to be made as widely available as possible through the production of homiletic and exegetical material, both ancient and contemporary, as well as through the teaching of rhetorical and theological methods for applying the texts to life.

Patristic exegesis was shaped by certain presuppositions which continued to inform the hermeneutics of the early medieval period. The fathers presupposed, first of all, that the Bible was a unified whole to which the interpretive key was the person, work and message of Christ. Christ was the fullness of salvation and the soteriological project of God was *the* mystery which was not just

---

[65] Also like some of them, Dhuoda composed her own epitaph. Riché notes the examples of Alcuin and Hincmar of Rheims.

revealed in the Scriptures but made present, as well, when the Scriptures were proclaimed. *Mystery* is to be understood as the whole intent of God for the salvation of the cosmos, beginning with creation and preliminarily revealed through creation, but only fully realized and revealed in the death and resurrection of Christ. This divine intent was expressed in all its saving power in the liturgical proclamation of the Scriptures. Therefore, an exposition of the Scriptures was done from the perspective of the presence and power of the proclaimed mystery in the life of the one who heard. As Tad Guzie says, in explaining the difference between patristic and modern critical exegesis, "Patristic exegesis takes as its starting point the Christian's relation to the mystery of which the text speaks. Thus scientific exegesis begins with a text which speaks of a mystery; patristic spiritual exegesis begins with the mystery spoken of in the text."[66] It is this starting point which leads the classical exegetes into the use of the complex of methods which can draw out the meaning of this mystery in the life of the believer, including typology, allegory and *theoria*. Whatever the differences and nuances between the meaning and application of these different methodological terms, the goal of their use was to illuminate this "spiritual" (or "mystical," from *musterion*) meaning of the text. Thus understood, the "spiritual" sense of Scripture does not mean merely its ascetical implications but its power to realize and to enact the full mystery of divine salvation in the life of the believing community.

A second presupposition, dependent on the first, is that the scriptural texts contain a range of possible meanings, limited to some degree by what contemporary exegetes would call the historical meaning of the text, but broader and more inclusive of those applications which the on-going experience of the Christian community would both require and expose. History grounds and shapes the range of possible meanings, but the meaning of the text is not exhausted by the history of the events it narrates; it

---

[66] "Patristic Hermeneutics and the Meaning of Tradition," *TS* 32, 1971, 649.

encompasses the experiences and new situations that arise out of the history of the reader.[67] To read the texts in the light of the concrete situations of one's own day is not to impose meaning, but to elicit it from the full, rich treasury of the text. We see this implicitly in Jerome, explicitly in Gregory the Great and Bede. It is inherent in the commentaries of Augustine and in the doctrinal expositions of Irenaeus and Athanasius (and, of course, in the sermons of all good preachers). The particular hermeneutic relationship between reader and text that Burton-Christie identifies with the desert dwellers of the early monastic movement was, in fact, inherent in the classical exegetical tradition as a whole. What he says about the ideal of holiness conceived of in the desert describes the way in which Scripture was understood to inform all forms of Christian life; it "meant giving concrete shape to the world of possibilities stretching ahead of the sacred texts by interpreting them and appropriating them into one's life."[68]

Given this understanding of biblical interpretation and application, it is not surprising that the *tradition of interpretation* became increasingly important. The history of the believing community is reflected in the living exegetical tradition; those who interpret the Scriptures for their particular community express the saving mystery still unfolding in new times and new places. Later

---

[67] This understanding of all texts as polysemous is, of course, central to the contemporary conversation about hermeneutics. In addition to the deconstructionists such as Derrida, Barthes and Eco who have taken a prominent role in this conversation, David Tracy, Paul Ricoeur and Hans-Georg Gadamer have proposed positions in the company of which Dhuoda's understanding would not be considered entirely naive or pre-critical. See, e.g., David Tracy, *The Analogical Imagination: Christian Theology and the Culture of Pluralism* (New York: Crossroads, 1986), 115–24.

[68] Douglas Burton-Christie, *The Word in the Desert: Scripture and Quest for Holiness in Early Christian Monasticism* (New York and Oxford: Oxford University Press, 1993), 20. Dhuoda paraphrases a story from the *Verba Seniorum* in one place in the text (as noted by Riché, 316, n. 2), demonstrating that she had some acquaintance with that fount of spiritual wisdom (VIII, 13, 34–46).

exegetes would come to rely on earlier exegesis because it suggested some of the possible meanings inherent in the sacred text and pointed to the ways in which that meaning could be extended. During periods of theological aridity, it is true, the great exegetes of the first five centuries were simply copied, often in almost unintelligible fragments, as later Christians attempted to maintain the biblical life of their communities. But even in the "dark ages," exegetes such as Bede could re-vivify the tradition by bringing their own particular issues to bear upon the text, and by the Carolingian period, exegetes could approach the earlier material as a source of pertinent and provocative interpretations, capable of being restructured for new situations.[69] Undoubtedly the prestige of earlier exegetes such as Jerome, Augustine and Ambrose contributed to the value which later interpreters attributed to their work; they were saints and, quoted by official church teaching, they were the *doctores sacres*. Their status was important as was their use of Latin which made them accessible to later writers. But not all earlier interpretations were to be considered valid expressions of the saving mystery, not all were "within the tradition." Validity was determined by orthodoxy, which is to say that particular interpretations were to be tested by their congruence with the mystery understood as a whole. Irenaeus had very early enunciated this principle in *Against the Heresies* III. The tradition handed down from the Apostles through the visible episcopacy was to be the norm by which individual readings of the Scripture were measured.   According to Irenaeus, the coherent doctrine of salvation contained in the creeds enables even the barbarians to discriminate between the wisdom of the tradition and heretical "claptrap" (4.2)! The one who reads or hears can unlock the true meaning of the Scripture only if she does so with authentic faith in the whole mystery expressed in the creed. That creed was the essential hermeneutical framework accepted by the classical

---

[69] See Schneiders on the normative character of apostolic tradition and subsequent interpretation, 75–78.

authors as well as by Bede, Dhuoda and her contemporaries. These later practitioners continually learned the process of orthodox interpretation by allowing themselves to be guided by the masters of the tradition.

To read the Bible in this way requires its own methods. The legacy of Origen and Gregory the Great had made the four-fold allegorical interpretation a commonplace in the Carolingian period. But Origen, in systematizing the allegorical method, was refining, not inventing, since allegory is a development of the typology by which the New Testament writers themselves began the appropriation of the earlier biblical material and is therefore to be found in the New Testament itself. Origen notes Paul's use of the word *allegory* and patristic exegesis as a whole does not make a distinction, so important to contemporary scholars, between typology which acknowledges the importance of the historical meaning of the text and allegory which, today, is generally understood as a consequence of a neo-platonic reading. K. J. Woollcombe in his essay, "The Biblical Origins and Patristic Development of Typology," and G. W. H. Lampe in a companion piece entitled "The Reasonableness of Typology,"[70] distinguish between two types of typology, historical and philosophical. The first is rooted in the theological developments in later Israel and continues into the New Testament; "it consists in a recognition of historical correspondences" (30), as Lampe notes, and, as a method of "exegesis, is the search for linkages between events, persons or things within the historical framework of revelation. . . " (40), in the words of Woollcombe. For both of these writers, it is the close adherence to history which specifies this kind of typology, and the respect for history and for the historical meaning of the text gives

---

[70] Published together in *Essays on Typology*, Studies in Biblical Theology 22 (London: SCM Press, 1957).

it authenticity.[71] The typological imagination sees in the events and persons which are the instruments of salvation in the history of Israel patterns which anticipate the fullness of salvation brought by Christ and worked out within the life of the early faith communities. Typology is a method by which Old Testament events are seen as types or figures of the work of Christ; more than that, it is the theological understanding, rooted in a particular doctrine of God, of salvation as enacted and revealed in history.[72] This is the kind of interpretation which allows the church to understand the preparatory work of God in history and to see, for example, the story of Noah as an early anticipation of the salvation through water that is most fully realized in Christian baptism.

Lampe and Woollcombe find the roots of the second kind of typology in a neo-Platonic way of seeing the world and of reading texts; this is more generally called allegory. Often arbitrary and capricious in its application and frequently without a clear connection to the historical meaning of the text, allegory is, nonetheless, a reflection of the understanding that the visible and historical world stands to the world of the spirit as shadow to reality. Related more to the way educated Greeks had read Homer than to the way in which Jews had traditionally read the story of Exodus, allegorical typology tends to dissolve the textured

---

[71] Jean Danielou had made a similar distinction somewhat earlier, while Henri de Lubac, in dialogue with Danielou, cautioned against maintaining too rigid a distinction between historical typology and philosophical allegory in the works of the Fathers. See Walter J. Burghardt, S.J., "On Early Christian Exegesis," *TS* 11 (1950), 78–116. In the medieval period, however, the distinction is important. Lawrence T. Martin argues for it in "The Two Worlds in Bede's Homilies," *De Ore Domini: Preacher and Word in the Middle Ages* (Kalamazoo, MI: Medieval Institute Publications, 1989), 27–60; in looking at Dhuoda's work, I believe that the distinction allows for greater clarity.

[72] As G. W. H. Lampe says so well, "Yet this proleptic honour enjoyed by the events of the Old Testament in no way deprived them of straightforward historical reality; indeed it is their historicity that bestows upon them an evidential value denied to imaginative speculations," *Essays on Typology,* Studies in Biblical Theology 22 (London: SCM Press Ltd., 1957), 13.

specificity of biblical texts into abstractions of philosophical wisdom.[73] Such a reading often considers a single word or detail of the text, rather than a passage or event as a whole and is generally tailored to a particular practical or moral application. A classical bit of allegorical interpretation is found toward the end of the *DDC* where Augustine interprets the Jews taking the riches of the Egyptians in the Exodus as a justification for Christian scholars seizing all of the educational tools of the pagans for their own study of the Scripture.

Dhuoda's use of allegory in this philosophical sense is quite limited, especially if we distinguish philosophical allegory from other rhetorical devices such as numerology and etymology. She is aware of the way in which Christian exegetes consistently found a fuller sense in Old Testament passages; she speaks of those living in Old Testament times as having "seen" the image ("figura") of the Trinity in their encounters with the divine as if in a mirror.[74] Early in her text she indicates that she knows the various allegorical "senses" of patristic exegesis. Attempting to explain the title she has given her book, she gives a three-fold interpretation of the second part of the word *manualis* (handbook), saying that "although 'alis,' the ending of the first word of the title, has many meanings, here [she] will unfold only three of them according to certain opinions of the Fathers."[75] Occasionally, the allegorical method gives her a degree of freedom in putting forth her own interpretation. Knowing that patristic interpretation often seemed to distort the literal meaning of the text, she allows herself to give such an interpretation, though it seems to make her a bit

---

[73] Hellenistic Jews had already developed the method of philosophical allegory for their own reading of the Scriptures. Philo's contribution cannot be overlooked.

[74] "Multi autem ex eis, ante aduentum Domini et Saluatoris nostri Christi Ihesu, figuram Sanctae Trinitatis contemplantes quasi per speculum. . . " (II, 1, 10–12).

[75] "'Alis' quanquam multas habet significationes, tamen hoc in loco secundum quidem sententias Patrum tribus replicabo sensibus. . ." (Incipit, l. 26–28).

uncomfortable (whether because she feels inadequate or whether because she prefers the historical meaning is difficult to determine). Hence, in Book VII, in an extended interpretation of physical birth and death as a type of spiritual birth and death—which was, of course, a thoroughly traditional theme—she says, (quoting what she wrongly believes to be a Pauline saying) "though this passage actually means something else, for various good reasons, I want you to understand it here in the way I interpret it."[76] When she does essay an allegorical interpretation of her own, the results are generally not felicitous.   In her own use of the lovely line of Canticles 8:3, "His left hand under my head and his right hand shall embrace me," the left hand becomes "this present life, in which each one of us is bent with toil" and the right, "the holy and worthy homeland of heaven."[77] Even granted the often twisted allegorical interpretations given to the Book of Canticles, this is particularly arbitrary and flat.

Most often, Dhuoda simply takes a particular allegorical interpretation from her sources. Thus in I, 3, she uses the three-fold sense of "from the rising of the sun to its going down" (Ps 112:3) to indicate the parallel meaning of a single day, the extent of a human life and the entire span of human history, a common patristic theme, as Pierre Riché notes.[78] Like the fathers, and undoubtedly from their treasury, she takes allegorical meanings

---

[76] Et licet aliter hoc in loco uoluatur sensus, pro certis differentium causis, ego uolo ut ita teneas sicut fateor" (VII, 1, 16–18). See also (III, 10, 49–58), where she takes an admonitory text and turns it around, so that, as she says, it means something positive ("in bonam uertentes partem").

[77] "Quid in sinistra, fili, nisi praesens intelligitur uita, in qua unusquisque elaborando uoluitur nostrum? Et quid in dextera, nisi sancta et digna coelestis ostenditur patria?" (VI, 4, 53–56).

[78] *Manuel pour mon fils*, 103, n. 4. See also the use of the "dew of Hermon" and the oil on the head of Aaron as images of the blessing of God (also a commonplace of allegorical interpretation).

from the world of natural history.[79] Etymologies form a distinct rhetorical strategy for unlocking the meaning of scriptural words, but they are related to allegory and often spill over into it. In III, 11, for instance, Dhuoda's interpretation of the role of priests and the kinds of reverence due to them is a grand mixture of etymologies and allegories taken, most likely, from Isidore, Alcuin and Augustine. Dhuoda's fondness for etymologies and her fascination with numerology and computation[80] reveal the pedagogical methods she would have been exposed to,[81] but they also show her respect for the work, in particular, of Augustine and Isidore of Seville. In sum, Dhuoda's use of what Lampe and Woolcombe designate as philosophical allegory is primarily a result of her reliance on her sources; her individual attempts are sporadic and, at best, awkward.

But an historical understanding of typology grounds virtually all of Dhuoda's use of the Bible. We see it in the way in which she applies the story of the Syro-Phoenician woman to herself and all other believers who, in her own day, gather under the table of the Lord to scramble for the falling crumbs of divine wisdom. It is demonstrated by the way in which she uses a plethora of Old Testament characters as models of political and social behavior for her sons and his peers. It grounds her use of the Psalms as her own prayers. Typology is, most importantly, the theological basis for the sense of salvation history that pervades Dhuoda's text and many of her contemporaries' texts as well. She demonstrates a conscious conviction that the history of salvation encompassed all of human history. This is revealed in I, 3 where she underlines the parallel between a single day, a human life and the full sweep of history, making explicit that this history flows from the creation of Adam to the death of the last human being at the end of time. Again, in

---

[79] See, for example, the extended allegory of the harts (III, 10, 80–116).

[80] See, in particular, I, 5 and IX, 1–4.

[81] Riché has noted this: 187, n. 9.

IX, 4, she writes, "We believe that all those who are saved, from the creation to the end of the world, will be collected to restore the tenth angelic order under the law as I have said before," thus enlarging the notion of salvation history to include a cosmic teleology. She borrows this idea from Augustine and Gregory the Great[82] but it seems personally important to her since she repeats it.

Indeed, history, inclusively understood as salvation history, is a special concern of the Carolingians. Some of the most important chronicles and annals which proliferate during the ninth century are being written even as Dhuoda herself writes. What J. M. Wallace-Hadrill finds remarkable in the work of Hincmar is present, with some modification, in the *Liber Manualis*. She too found in the Books of Kings the lesson that a nation prospered to the extent that its rulers submitted to the divine economy; she too sees the past as a useful continuum in which biblical ancestors and past family members are equally important models of responsible aristocratic conduct. Like Hincmar, Dhuoda "intends to leave a picture of public life in the widest sense, the triumphs, betrayals and misunderstandings of the men [s]he knew. And all this [s]he views against the purposes of God for the society [s]he belonged to."[83] Very clearly for Dhuoda, salvation history is personal, continued in her own family. The careful attention she gives to drawing up William's genealogy is echoed by the way in which she repeatedly refers to Old Testament personages as "our" or "your ancestors in the faith." One may deduce from her text that the classical hermeneutic problem of the Christian use of the Old Testament is resolved for her, not so much by the allegorical interpretation put

---

[82] See Riché, 333, n. 3. "De protoplasto usque in ultimum qui in fine mundi saluandus est, ad hoc eos credimus esse colligendos, ut decimus, sicut praedixi, legaliter recuperetur ordo angelicus" (2-5).

[83] "History in the Mind of Archbishop Hincmar," *The Writing of History in the Middle Ages*, R. H. C. Davis and J. M. Wallace-Hadrill (Oxford: Clarendon Press, 1981), 59.

forth by Origen, but by this sense of personalized history. The Old Testament books, particularly the narratives, are in no way alien from her faith and theological experience. Separated from her *only in time*, the religious experience of Israel and the revelation it transmits are hers by a kind of familial inheritance. The theological continuity presumed by typology is reinforced by historical continuity; the Kings of Israel, as well as her prophets, poets and bearers of wisdom, are part of William's spiritual genealogy and of the inheritance he is bequeathed as an adopted child of God.

Lampe and Woollcombe pay slight attention to the typological use of texts inherent in the liturgical use of biblical texts from the beginning of the Christian period.[84] But in its liturgical context, typology had three terms: 1) prefigurement, 2) fulfillment, 3) actualization in the worshipping community. The salvation that was prefigured in Old Testament event and fully expressed in the New was made actual in the readings and rituals of the particular believing community assembled for liturgical worship. Jean Danielou, S.J. points out the essential connection between these three terms.

But these eschatological times [in which O.T. figures are fulfilled] are not only those of the life of Jesus, but of the church as well. Consequently the eschatological typology of the Old Testament is accomplished not only in the person of Christ, but also in the church. Besides Christological typology, therefore, there exists a sacramental typology. . . this means furthermore that the sacraments carry on in our midst the *mirabilia*, the great works of God in the Old Testament and the New. . . . [85]

---

[84] Paul F. Bradshaw has developed this theme in "The Use of the Bible in Liturgy: Some Historical Perspectives," *SL* 22 (1992), 35–52.

[85] *The Bible and the Liturgy* (Notre Dame, IN: University of Notre Dame Press, 1956), 5.

A typological understanding of liturgical texts and action gathers the later Christian community, when assembled for sacred action, into the full flow of salvation history since liturgy is concerned with the immediate appropriation of the sacred realities attested to by the texts. Inasmuch as liturgical action is prepared for and completed by Christian life outside the assembly, it was an easy step to view all of life itself as part of the panoramic flow of salvation history. Historical typology, particularly as experienced in a liturgical context, collapses to some degree the hermeneutical distance between the reader and the world of the biblical text; the world of past salvific events becomes not just a moral ideal to be striven for, but a present reality to be embraced. Thus typology, especially as nuanced by liturgical reading of the texts, helps to form the theological basis for understanding the biblical text within the specific context of one's own life and history. Liturgical or sacramental typology requires that one take human history very seriously indeed and the understanding of salvation as history is not limited to its past expressions, for it is the continual ground for both human existence and divine activity. Though this understanding was particularly important within the monastic tradition where liturgical reading and personal reading were intimately intertwined, it was also a critical element in all of the exegesis of the early medieval period. The Scripture was, on the one hand, the expression of the full mystery of salvation (understood within the ecclesial community); on the other hand, the reading of Scripture, whether in liturgical assembly or privately, was the occasion of the deep encounter with that mystery in personal experience, the condition of its understanding.

Influences of the liturgy are quite visible in Dhuoda's *Liber Manualis*. She ends her acrostic verses with a reference to the liturgical season which is unfolding as she completes her book, "as December is beginning, on the feast of St. Andrew, during the season of the Coming of the Word."[86] There are a number of

---

[86] "Incohans december, Andreae sancti festa,/ Aduentus Verbi" (X, 2, 72–73).

references to the canonical hours, that monastic structure of prayer which was understood as the model for the daily prayer of all Christians, and to the practice of which Dhuoda bids William attend.[87] The Good Friday intercessions influence the model prayers she constructs for William's use.[88] She speaks of the efficacy of masses offered for the dead[89] and she gives some of our earliest evidence for the use of the sign of the cross as an extra-liturgical practice.[90] We are not surprised, therefore, to find in her understanding of the Scriptures an emphasis upon the living and actual presence of the saving mystery to be found there. She says explicitly: "God's word is living. Search it eagerly."[91] In the many places in which she speaks of reading the Scriptures, she insists that personal and practical experience will illuminate the text; scriptural knowledge of God is made possible through self-knowledge (a theme that pervades the tradition, particularly after Augustine). As she says in explaining the process of meditation, "When once you have begun to consider who or what God is, how great and of what quality, you will discover your inability to understand God fully or find God's equal. Then you will know—through the very inability to know—that this one alone is God."[92] Because the Scripture is the living and active presence of God, the dynamics of reading and the dynamics of prayer are almost identical. What Dhuoda says so often about reading, she says also about prayer, that it is a reality involving mouth, heart and

---

[87] II, 3, 77–80; VIII, 15, 10–12; XI, 1, 1.

[88] Book VIII, chaps 2–8. See Riché, 307, n. 4 and 311, n. 4.

[89] VIII, 16, 3–5.

[90] II, 3, 45–52. See Riché 129, n. 5 and Neel, 120, n. 29.

[91] "Est uiuus sermo Dei: illum perquire; . . " (X, 2, 6).

[92] "Nam, cum coeperis considerare quis, quantus aut qualis sit, et non poteris comprehendere uel invenire cooperatorem similem illi, scies per omnia quia hoc est Deus" (I, 5, 55–58).

action. "Pray with your mouth, cry out in your heart, beg by your action, that God may support you always, . . ."[93]

If history is a primary hermeneutic category for Dhuoda, then action is another and its correlative,[94] reinforced by the way in which history became action in liturgy. She never tires of repeating to William that he must read, internalize and enact the words that he finds in Scripture, in classical writings and in her own text. Reading is incomplete without action; learning is a matter of intellectual understanding that arises from personal experience and the practice of what one reads and, subsequently, flows into right action.[95] In Book I, for instance, when she begins to expose the mystery of God, she writes to William, "I admonish you continually to mull over the words of the holy gospels and the writings of the fathers concerning these [things]. . . . By thinking, speaking and acting rightly, you may believe in the everlasting God, who remains one in trinity and triune in unity."[96] Here Dhuoda makes explicit her understanding of what true meditation is: it is the extended

---

[93] "Ora ore, clama corde, roga opere, ut tibi Deus succurat semper. . ." (II, 3, 32–33).

[94] Paul Ricoeur has investigated, from a contemporary perspective, the importance of action in the hermeneutic process. See "The Model of the Text: Meaningful Action Considered as a Text," in *Hermeneutics and the Human Sciences*, ed., trans., intro. J. Thompson (Cambridge: Cambridge University Press, 1981).

[95] As Burton-Christie notes (with reference to both Gadamer and Tracy, "The recognition that the risk of interpretation can bring about transformation suggests the importance of praxis or *applicatio*. It has been noted that *applicatio* is intrinsic, not extrinsic to interpretation. This means that interpretation, if it is to be complete, must be understood as always involving praxis and leading to some form of transformation," 23.

[96] "Hoc te admoneo ut et in uirtutes, et in elementa, et in corporis sensu<s>, dicta sanctorum euangeliorum, cum aliorum documenta Patrum in tua semper reuoluas mente, ut unum in trinitate et trinum in unitate, bene cogitando, bene loquendo, bene operando, sine fine posse credas manentem ipsum qui dicitur Deus" (I, 5, 42–47).

process, "in tua semper reuoluas mente" (which Neel translates "to ponder in your heart") in which thinking flows into speaking (whether prayer or discourse is not clear) that, in turn, becomes action. This three-step process leads to authentic faith which is not merely an understanding of God, but union with and possession of the divine reality. In Book II, 2, on the theological virtues, she bids William to seek and to find all the goods appropriate to him—earthly goods certainly, but heavenly goods as well, of which the chief good is God. "God is the one from whom you hope to receive all good things: desire God by thinking, ask in word, and move toward God in your actions. By acting in this three-fold manner, you will arrive at the height of perfection which is called charity."[97] The goal of reading is a virtuous understanding; the text is not just words about God but the power of God for salvation. Its full meaning is not to be had by study alone (though Dhuoda insists repeatedly that study is the irreplaceable first step) but by the habitual practice of what is read.

This is the classical understanding of the relationship between Scripture, life and salvation. It is the medieval variant of the "hermeneutical circle"[98] which became a permanent legacy of the western church through the monastic practice of *lectio divina* and was intrinsic to the hermeneutic tradition from the late classical period to scholasticism. The integral role which transformed *praxis* plays in Dhuoda's hermeneutics suggests a (very limited) comparison with certain latter-day theologians. The thought of someone like Juan Luis Segundo can illuminate the way in which early medieval writers genuinely anticipate certain contemporary

---

[97] "A quo bona cuncta speras accipere, quaere cogitando, pete loquendo, pulsa operando. Haec tria agendo ad summam et perfectam uevies, quae dicitur karitas" (II, ii, 29–31).

[98] See Richard J. Bernstein, *Beyond Objectivism and Relativism: Science, Hermeneutics and Praxis* (Phila: University of Pennsylvania Press, 1983), especially Parts Two and Three, for a general discussion of the relationship between *praxis* and interpretation in the contemporary debate.

questions even while it clarifies the wide gulf between them. In *Liberation of Theology*,[99] Segundo preliminarily defines the hermeneutic circle as "the continuing change in our interpretation of the Bible which is dictated by the continuing changes in our present-day reality, both individual and societal." Certainly this describes the conviction that drives Dhuoda's interpretation: at every step she uses the concrete realities of her life situation (and William's) to elicit a specific and practical meaning of the text. On the other hand, Segundo's *preconditions* for the hermeneutic circle arise out of a critical mindset foreign to Dhuoda and her world. He speaks of "ideological" and "exegetical suspicions" that the prevailing theology has been warped by its adherence to past social realities. Dhuoda's "suspicion" (if it can be called that) is that prevailing theology has not, as yet, mined fully the richness of meaning contained in the sacred text. Segundo's hermeneutics is designed to deconstruct earlier interpretations; Dhuoda wants to expand them. Both, however, find their starting point in the here-and-now and in a commitment to *praxis*. In his contrast between "the traditional academic theologian" and "the liberation theologian," Segundo reveals that, for him "traditional" theology began with scholasticism and takes place, almost exclusively, in the schools. The "traditional theology" against which Dhuoda works is formulated by bishops and monks for specific communities of faith, not unlike those Segundo seeks to address. Like Segundo and other liberation theologians as well, Dhuoda's biblical interpretation has always a strong moral character. If theology is "faith seeking understanding," then Dhuoda's theology posits action as the very condition of understanding. Her theology takes its agenda from the world of action and emphasizes action as the way to faith.

Inevitably, then, Dhuoda's moral discourse will turn to political realities, issues of great concern to the better-known theologians such as Rhaban Maur and Hincmar of Rheims as well as to Dhuoda. The great theologians of the classical period did not, of

---

[99] (Maryknoll: Orbis Books, 1988), 8.

course, hesitate to draw out in some detail the implications of the gospel ethic for the practical concerns particularly of wealth and poverty, the ownership of property and usury.[100] But in the context of a new imperial self-understanding, the need to develop a biblical and coherent understanding of the Christian commonwealth drew much attention from all those, bishops and abbots, who were responsible for the renewal of the church and state alike. Born out of Carolingian statecraft and the sometimes desperate need of the emperors for legitimation of their policy, this theological task would go beyond the merely pragmatic issue of the moment, and encompass prophetic-critical elements as well. Dhuoda participates in this aspect of the theological dialogue of her day, developing the teaching of the beatitudes into a treatise on William's social and political responsibilities as a member of the ruling class and formulating a theological understanding of the political position of the royal counsellor.

Typology is the principle by which Dhuoda can interpret her situation in biblical categories, respecting both the history of the text and her own. Action is an existential entrée into the text and a test of one's own interpretation of it. Finally, however, the interpretation of particular passages becomes coherent only if understood against a specific theological horizon: the entire mystery of salvation communicated by biblical revelation and understood in an ecclesial context, the traditional test of orthodoxy. Therefore, it is important to recognize that all of Dhuoda's particular teaching in the *Liber Manualis* is set within a cohesive theological framework

---

[100] See Carolyn Osiek, *Rich and Poor in the Shepherd of Hermas: An Exegetical-Social Investigation* (Washington, DC: The Catholic Biblical Association, 1983), *The Rich Christian in the Church of the Early Empire. Contradictions and Accommodations,* Texts and Studies in Religions (New York and Toronto: Edwin Mellen Press, 1980); John G. Gager, *Kingdom and Community: The Social World of Early Christianity* (Englewood Cliffs, NJ: Prentice-Hall, 1975); Martin Hengel, *Property and Riches in the Early Church: Aspects of a Social History of Early Christianity,* trans. John Bowden (Philadelphia: Fortress Press, 1974); Abraham J. Malherbe, *Social Aspects of Early Christianity* (Baton Rouge: Louisiana State University, 1977).

and to note the way in which she expresses her understanding of the Christian salvific mystery as a whole.[101] She begins her own exposition of the broad outlines of the faith with an exposition of who and what God is, the trinitarian nature of God, the human need to search for God and the relationship between God and the human person as it is constructed upon the three theological virtues and prayer.

At the beginning of her text comes a portrait of God, the ultimate feudal lord. Like the feudal lord's, God's power is based on relationship with the land. Feudal theory held that the land belonged entirely to the sovereign and was allotted to members of the nobility in return for service. As Dhuoda points out, God is the final and absolute sovereign whose ownership of the land is based on creation. As she says, "He is the God of the universe; to him belong power and kingdom and empire." [102] God's sovereignty is that upon which all human sovereignty is based and, though human power brings with it the illusion of ownership, this illusion is soon exposed in the ups and downs of human fortune. The king may take away the honors and land he has conferred and, even if he doesn't, all ownership ends with death.

> . . . we on earth say (and they say) 'this is mine; all of it is.'
> They speak truly, of course, because it is and yet it isn't.
> These things pass away and they remain; they belong to

---

[101] She seems particularly concerned that William grasp and retain the orthodox expressions of the faith and regularly enjoins him to read "the orthodox fathers." She says in Book II, 1, for instance, "Read the volumes of the orthodox fathers and you will find out what the Trinity is." (Lege uolumina ortodoxorum Patrum, et quid sit Trinitas inuenies), 5–6.

[102] "Deus uniuersorum ipse est; ipsius est potestas regnumque et imperium" (I, 5, 92–93).

someone for a little while but not forever; they pass away at the right moment but not in every moment.[103]

Human dominion is real, but it is both transient and contingent. God is the only permanent sovereign whose dominion lasts forever.

At the same time, God the Creator is God the Redeemer. The munificence of creation is the ground of Christian hope that God can and will bring weak human beings to perfection.[104] God is not only the sovereign lord who stands outside the human condition; God is effectively present within the very fabric of human existence. This conviction unifies her understanding of the Christian mystery and grounds her moral theology in a specific theology of God. A passage at the end of Book I, 6, brings together some of the metaphoric richness of her understanding of God in a synthesis that is personal, passionate and significant.

> Believe that he is above you, below you, within and outside of you; he is the over-arching reality, the foundation, the interior reality and the reality outside. He is the reality above because he presides over and rules us all. He is on high and, as the psalmist says, "his glory is above all the heavens." He is the foundation because he bears us up: "in him we live, we move, we have our being, and in him we take our stand." He is the interior reality because we are filled with him, the source of all good things, yes, filled to satiation as the Scripture says: "With the fruit of your

---

[103] "Ista contendentes in saeculo dicimus et dicunt: 'Meum est, et cuncta'. Verum dicunt quia est et non est, abent et non abent, est ad modicum sed non semper, abent ad tempus sed non omne tempus" (I, 5, 76–79).

[104] After describing God's creative power in words taken from the Book of Job, Dhuoda concludes, "Et si talis est et talia cuncta per saecula regit, potest et tuum, o amantissime fili Wilhelme, ad culmen perfectionis deducere statum, nutrireque et crescere ad maius" (I, 5, 52–55). This soteriological theme perdures through the theological tradition from Paul, through Irenaeus and is found in the fourteenth century text of Julian of Norwich as well.

works the earth is filled and you fill every creature with blessing." He is the reality around us because his impregnable wall surrounds us all; he makes us secure, protects and defends us. As it is written: "He circles us with a wall and like a shield he spreads his encircling care."[105]

Her imagination moves her thought from the Ruler God above to the sustaining God, the "ground of our being," below, from the God who is the living interior spring to the exterior encircling wall. The God who is the center of Dhuoda's thought is indeed beyond the limits of her intellectual understanding; but her imagination grasps a reality that escapes and exceeds the feudal images with which she consciously grapples.

Her book on the search for God is followed by some chapters on the Trinity and the theological virtues. Dhuoda seems greatly concerned that William's understanding of this central Christian teaching be completely orthodox. Undoubtedly this is a reflection of the trinitarian controversies that had divided the Carolingian kingdom in the previous century, and Dhuoda's thought contributes nothing original. She repeats the traditional use of Old Testament types as well as the allegorical interpretations of texts from the Old Testament and from Paul. True to her central purpose, which is the personal appropriation of Christian truth by her son, she interests herself primarily in *eliciting faith* in the Trinity and *affection* for the three persons who, though distinct in personhood, are one in divine nature. For Dhuoda, this is the *saving truth* which William must

---

[105] "Crede eum supra, subtus, infra et extra; ipse est enim superior, subterior, interior et exterior. Superior, quia omnes nos praesidet et regit. Ipse est excelsus, et, ut ait Psalmista, super omnes coelos gloria eius. Supterior, quia omnes nos portat: in illo uiuimus, mouemur et sumus, et in illo subsistimus semper. Interior quia omnes nos bonis suis replet et satiat, ut scriptum est: De fructu operum tuorum satiabitur terra; et reples omne animal benedictione. Exterior, quia omnes nos muro suo inexpugna-bili circumcingit, munit, protegit ac defendit, ut scriptum est: Muro cingit et in modum scuti inducit coronam" (I, 6, 19–33).

have to avoid the "fiery furnace." Even in her discussion of the Trinity, it is soteriology rather than theodicy that concerns her. Her image of God inevitably shapes her understanding of Christian life. Speaking of the theological virtues which, by definition, make the human person capable of divine communication, she is at pains to point out the intrinsic relationship between an appreciation of this world and the ability to apprehend the supernatural world. Although throughout the *Liber* she insists thematically upon the transitory nature of this world and all that it prizes, she is convinced that this world is not *unimportant* in the pursuit of the Kingdom of God. She points out to William that the natural virtue of hope teaches him to hope for the eternal realities. For her, the principle of analogy is an important theological reality.

> Earthly realities such as these, my son, teach us about heavenly ones. When you have moved the world and acquired what you wanted, you will rejoice as is the custom of the world. I exhort you that your seeking and acquiring be not limited to the here and now but be directed also to the future . . . Go after earthly things, but long for the eternal.[106]

For Dhuoda, a proper perspective on the world—seeing it for the transitory reality that it is—will enhance one's joy in this life. There is a deep and essential continuity between both worlds. Earthly realities teach about heavenly ones; the proper use and enjoyment of earth is a necessary step to heaven. Especially is this true of William and the class to which he belongs; upon the nobility depended the civil peace that is the expression and necessary context for the kingdom of the Prince of Peace. That kingdom comes, in Dhuoda's mind, not only after earthly kingdoms

---

[106] "Docent, fili, terrena quae sunt coelestia. Tu cum pulsaueris in saeculo et adquisieris, gaudebis, sicut mos est; ortor te et admoneo ut petitio uel adquisieristio tua sit non solum hic, sed etiam in futuro; . . . Petes ista, quaere illa" (II, 2, 13–18).

disappear, but also to the degree that earthly kingdoms are faithful to the gospel. Charity, the most sublime of the theological virtues, is a matter of making choices. To choose God is to go beyond earthly things; but to truly come to God, one must choose and act in relation to the world in which one lives. The vertical dimension of Christian life in no way eclipses but rather enhances the horizontal; salvation is not merely "pie in the sky" but "daily bread" as well.

For Dhuoda, human life is a journey toward the Kingdom of God, a journey which engages the seeker of that Kingdom in responsible action in the world. The journey metaphor was completely traditional; Augustine gave it clear articulation and his thought was central to the thinking of the whole of medieval theology. However, the journey metaphor takes on new life in this Carolingian text from its prominence in the contemporary social situation; in their world knights were in continual movement from one battle to another, in constant visitation of their multiple outposts and territorial seats.[107]   Dhuoda never envisions this journey as an isolated one; hers is a communal understanding of human life in which the goal is to be welcomed into the community of the saints. Nor is the journey one which can be accomplished quickly. Her understanding of human perfection and the redemption of society is progressive. Perfection and peace come only at the end of a long life, in which one struggles continually. As she herself says, "everyone of us ought to choose such a way of life among the vicissitudes of these days that we may be free at the end."[108] Words denoting 'to make progress', 'to run', 'to grow', 'to mature' are sprinkled liberally throughout the text. The moral program she suggests to William, principally in Book IV, is built upon an understanding of human maturation that moves outward

---

[107] Dhuoda's husband, Bernard, seems only to have been with her for two extended periods during her almost twenty years of marriage.

[108] "Nam unusquisque nostrum . . . talem sibi, infra fluctuationes saeculi huius, eligere debet conuersationem, ut in finem liberari possit" (IV, 4, 20–23).

from interiority, developing from self-conquest to social action. His Christian heritage obliges him to fulfill his social duties in a way that is consonant with the gospel: seeing justice accomplished in the court, using military action to achieve peace and ensuring that the poor, the weak and the needy do not fall through the cracks of a social system built on wealth and power. The Christian's journey to perfection is to be structured according to the liturgical and spiritual life of the church. Dhuoda bids William pray according to the general format of the liturgy of the hours and when, at the end of the *Liber*, she gives a detailed list of appropriate prayers to be said for various categories of people, her instructions read as a kind of detailed gloss upon the litanies of the church. Dhuoda also refers William to the sacramental structure of the church, mentioning the value of auricular confession and the sacrifice of the mass. There is, however, and in spite of the liturgical influences on her writing, surprisingly little attention to the church as an institution and to ecclesiastical structures. Hers is a theological understanding of Christian life as an enterprise lived entirely within the soteriological mystery. She seems much less concerned about the forms of piety (though she recommends them) and about the institutional structures of salvation (though she assumes them) than about William's personal appropriation of the great mystery of salvation which, she believes, will come about through biblical study and right action.

This brings us to consider some of the other elements missing in the work o Carolingian author. Much that was of interest to imperial religion finds no place in Dhuoda's text. Carolingian scholars such as Thomas Head and Julia Smith have noted the importance of saints' relics and hagiographical texts in the work of court theologians and f this important bishops.[109] They note the interest of Louis the Pious in having a life of St. Denis as well as the concern of Charles the Bald's wife to find the relics of St.

---

[109] Thomas Head, "Carolingian Bishops and the Cult of the Holy" and Julia Smith, "Carolingians and the Holy," papers given at the International Medieval Institute, Kalamazoo, MI, May, 1991.

Scholastica. They further document a concern to use holy power, the power of the saints, to buttress the imperial power and the imperial desire to control the proliferation of saints, channeling their power in support of imperial power and clerical hierarchy. In contrast, Dhuoda has little interest in the development of institutional forms of power or in the development of the clergy. Her interest in the lives of the saints is, again, pastoral and ascetical. She quotes from the apocryphal Passion of Peter to support her convictions about humility (IV, 4, 11–14) and the Passion of St. Symphorianus to speak of the need to keep God and God's reign always before one's eyes (I, 7, 34f). Additionally, in her extended justification of herself as a teacher (VII, 3), she uses material from the Passion of Sts. Julianus, Basilissa and companions as well as that of St. Symphorianus (both texts well disseminated in Carolingian times) to buttress her own power! She uses the stories of the mothers of these martyr-saints to show the pertinence and importance of mothers' teaching the faith to their children.

What may be more surprising is the absence of any significant attention to the Virgin Mary in Dhuoda's *Liber*. Though the liturgical developments and codifications that took place during the Carolingian period gave a prominent place to Marian feasts and though homilies for these feasts began to proliferate, Dhuoda ignores these sources. Carolingian homilies suggest a number of ways in which Mary might have been of ascetical interest to spiritually minded Carolingians and, thus, pertinent to the themes Dhuoda developed.[110] She might well have been expected to have

---

[110] See, for instance, Mary Clayton, *The Cult of the Virgin Mary in Anglo-Saxon England* (Cambridge: The University Press, 1990). Clayton says: "The main con- tribution of the Carolingians to Mariological thinking was probably the greater emphasis they placed upon the person of Mary. Whereas patristic writers concentrated on Mary's role as Mother of God and its consequences for Christological doctrine, the Carolingians sought rather to explore the consequences for Mary herself. The Marian issues treated in the early Anglo-Saxon texts were also substantially developed by the Carolingian writers. From

recourse to Mary and her role in the life of the Savior, especially when she wanted to justify her own more active role in her sons' lives (as she used the various Passion accounts of the saints). Instead she quotes Mary's Magnificat in two places, without referring to the person of Mary at all. In III, 10, 15–16, she reminds William that he is to attend to the counsel of the lesser born because the Lord himself has "exalted the humble" and again, in II, 2, 24–26, she exhorts William to pray ardently for the virtue of hope and, indeed, to live in hope, because God "fills the hungry with good things." The biblical words of Mary find a small place in Dhuoda's teaching, but Mary herself is virtually absent.[111]

Evidently, Dhuoda is selective in her appropriation of the theological and ascetical wisdom available to her and to her contemporaries. Though she repeatedly refers William to the reading of the "fathers" (by which she means both scriptural and authoritative Christian authors), she has selected from the storehouse of that tradition only that which suits her purpose and her methods. Her understanding of God—creator and savior, lord and companion, transcendent and immanent—is mediated through her own personal and social experience. In turn, this image shapes her anthropology and the principles by which she selects the material for her son's handbook. Her own reading of Scripture, a reading that begins with her personal experience and is designed to illuminate that experience, forms warp and woof of the *Liber Manualis*. It is to an analysis of that reading of Scripture that we now turn our attention.

---

being little more than a necessary factor in the life of Christ, Mary had, by the Carolingian period, become a figure of importance in her own right" 23.

[111] Riché finds a possible reference to Mary in the Epigrams at the beginning of the book. "Est tamen michi consors amica/ Fidaque, de tuis relaxandi crimina" Epigramme, 30–31 (p. 74). If this is such a reference, the appeal is to Mary as the mediatrix of graces for the sinful Christian, a theme which was in evidence in the ninth century, but not fully developed until the twelfth.

Chapter Three

THE SYRO-PHOENICIAN WOMAN

Dhuoda's *Liber Manualis* exemplifies some of the problems and possibilities of biblical interpretation as it was understood and practiced in the ninth century. Her use of the Bible is varied and cohesive. Her interpretation of particular passages and biblical figures raises significant questions about the transmission and dissemination of the tradition, the role of the Bible in the personal lives of the laity, and the vitality of biblical exegesis in a period marked by scarcity of resources and what some have called a slavish devotion to patristic interpretations. In this chapter we will examine the use that Dhuoda makes of the story of the Syro-Phoenician woman (Matt 14: 21–28; Mk 7:24–30) in light of its antecedents in the Latin Christian tradition.[112] This text is of particular interest in the work of Dhuoda because she uses it in self-justification for her work as a teacher of Divine Wisdom. An exploration of the exegetical tradition that precedes her will enable us to determine whether or not there is precedent for such use of the text within the tradition. It will also enable us to notice the way in which the historical context and concrete situation of the exegete influenced the interpretation even within the constraints imposed by a hermeneutic committed to past texts and traditional interpretations.

---

[112] I use the phrase "Syro-Phoenician woman" throughout for consistency, though, to be accurate, she is designated in the Marcan parallel as "the Canaanite woman."

Questions and Methods

Our first task is to lay down the questions and methods by which Dhuoda's interpretation can be situated within the textual and hermeneutical tradition that preceded her. One question concerns the possible liturgical context in which Dhuoda might have heard and appropriated this gospel pericope. The data about such liturgical influences comes from the lectionary manuscript tradition; the critical issue is the placement of the pericope in the lectionaries of the time. Lectionary data must also be compared with the Carolingian homiliaries which, though written to guide private study of the liturgical selections, give clues as to the actual pericopes used. A further question has to do with the methods which guided her use of the text. She is not writing a commentary nor an exegetical chain; by her own admission, she is not even attempting to write an organized treatise. By what process, then, did she arrive at the very personal interpretation we find in her use of the passage? The structure of the passage seems to indicate the kind of careful meditation known as *lectio divina* and can, I believe, be illuminated by the instructions laid down by Augustine in Book II of the *DDC*. Third, we can look at the specific exegetical tradition to which Dhuoda is likely to have had access, the Latin work of Jerome (who began as a translator of Origen and incorporated much of Origen in his own exegetical work) and Bede. Catalogs and other manuscript evidence contemporary with Dhuoda (as discussed in Chapter Two above) indicate the possibility that she knew these authors.

As far as liturgical influences are concerned, there are several ways in which Dhuoda gives the story of the Syro-Phoenician woman an explicitly Eucharistic flavor. She identifies the table in the original story with the Eucharistic altar, calling it the "table of the Lord;" she notes that to be under the table is to be inside holy church ('infra sanctam videlicet ecclesiam') where the ministers of the Lord gather around the altar. She interprets the bread which falls from the table as the word of God/true wisdom. The twofold identification of the eucharistic bread as both body of Christ and true wisdom of God was, by Dhuoda's time, a homiletic commonplace[113] that reflects the liturgical structure in which scriptural readings and the Eucharistic rite were celebrated in explicit parallel to each other. Further, she weaves fragments of two psalms (Pss 78 and 119 in modern editions) into her explication of the story in a manner distinctly reminiscent of the liturgical structure in which narratives are echoed by psalmodic responsorials. Ps 78 is an explicit reference to the sending of manna in the desert and reflects the connection just mentioned between Eucharistic bread and the bread of divine wisdom. This suggests at least the possibility that Dhuoda may have been influenced by the liturgical use of the pericope of the Syro-Phoenician woman.

However, the state of the lectionaries in use during her time, whether Roman, Gallican or Mozarabic, requires that this position be very carefully examined. A meticulous study of the sources (especially the work of Willis, Frere and Klauser), leads to nothing more than the suggestion of a possibility. During the critical period of development for the Roman rite, the story of the Syro-Phoenician woman was a kind of movable biblical feast. It was among the gospels technically given a place in the post-Epiphany period, but more probably was simply available for choice as an alternate reading for free days.[114] By 750, the pericope had moved

---

[113] Louis Bouyer finds two distinct traditions for the allegorical meaning of the manna/bread of life theme. "Although the whole Alexandrine tradition from Clement to Origen, following Philo, understands the manna to be a figure of the word of God following Matt IV: 4, the Eucharistic interpretation based on Jn VI: 31-33 is common in the catechesis." *Bible and Liturgy* (Notre Dame, IN: University of Notre Dame Press, 1964), 148. However, the use of these passages and others, like Matt 15: 21-28, in Eucharistic liturgies, would lead to a blending of these two meanings: the bread is both nourishment for our minds, enlightened by faith, and for our bodies, growing into immortality by participation in the bread of life.

[114] Walter Howard Frere, *The Roman Gospel-Lectionary, Studies in Early Roman Liturgy II* (Oxford: The University Press, 1934), 82-83.

into a more or less regular open spot, sometimes assigned to a free ferial day or Sunday during the first two weeks of Lent. In Bede's *Homilies on the Gospel,* for instance, it is located among a series of homilies "in Lent." The lectionary structure behind Bede's homilies has been identified as following the Neapolitan or Romano-Neapolitan usage.[115]   Ultimately the reading from Matt 15: 21–28 was assigned to the Thursday after the first Sunday of Lent, where it remained even after the Tridentine reform. Where rites other than the Roman prevailed, the position of the reading was even less fixed and less likely to be read than in the Roman rite. If Dhuoda had been influenced by the liturgical context, then, she would probably have been governed by its position in the Roman lectionary and might have been inclined to give the reading a Lenten, or penitential, nuance. But this is not the case. A liturgical *structure,* however, can be discerned within Dhuoda's use of the text.[116]   The rhythm of reading and response, the use of psalm or canticle verse to echo the major point of a narrative reading, was so thoroughly structured into all liturgical usage, whether in Mass, sacrament or Divine Office, that it became the way in which Christians generally read the biblical text. It underpins all later exegesis, especially the method known as *lectio divina.*

---

[115] Lawrence T. Martin, in his introduction to the English translation of Bede's homilies, notes that although Bede follows Gregory the Great's method and spirit and is also following his liturgical usage, Bede generally chooses to construct homilies on texts not treated by Gregory. The story of the Syro-Phoenician woman, then, was in the Neapolitan liturgical schema, but not a subject of Gregory's homilies. See *Bede the Venerable: Homilies on the Gospels,* trans. by Lawrence T. Martin and David Hurst, OSB (Kalamazoo, MI: Cistercian Publications, 1991), xvi–xvii. In CC 122, the homily is simply titled "In Quadragesima" and an editorial footnote indicates that no further specification is clear, although one thirteenth-century ms (Oxoniensis 176) carries the qualification "Cottidiana de Xlgessima feria VI," 156.

[116] See Appendix One for a schematic arrangement of the text which highlights the liturgical structure.

Though it is not generally acknowledged as such, a particular program of study laid out by Augustine in *DDC* perhaps formed a kind of bridge between the classical world of exegesis (done for the most part by bishops) and the variety of later methods (generally some form of *lectio divina*) by which bishop, monk, and lay Christian appropriated biblical texts for a multitude of personal and political reasons. In a short chapter from the *DDC*, a book which became the educational charter of the Middle Ages, Augustine describes a simple method for studying the Scriptures appropriate to the growing number among his readers for whom Latin was a second language and who would have had to struggle with the language of the biblical text before they confronted its theology. For those acquainted with the pedagogical tasks of the early ninth century, it is not hard to see Dhuoda and her contemporaries in the descriptions of Augustine. The text to which I refer is contained in Book II, Chapter 9 of the *DDC*.[117] It is a short passage and a dense one. Augustine begins it with a succinct statement that the method he proposes is for those who "in their devotion seek the will of God."[118] This is not a pious platitude, but a careful description of his audience. Though he expects careful, even rigorous, study, its purpose is not academic argumentation but a practical knowledge that leads to action. This is the express purpose of Dhuoda's reading of the Scriptures as well. She introduces her explanation of the pericope of the Syro-Phoenician woman by placing it in the context of the personal search for God. "You and I *must* search for God," she tells her son, "because we are placed within his will, and there we live, we move, we have our being."[119] Thus her intention

---

[117] I follow here the translation by John J. Gavigan in *Writings of Saint Augustine*, C 4 (New York: Cima Publishing, 1947). Citations are by page numbers.

[118] p. 71.

[119] "Quaerendus est Deus, fili, mihi et tibi; in illius nutu consistimus, uiuimus, mouemur et sumus" (I, 2, 2–3).

perfectly matches that of Augustine and his method can be discerned within her own text.

The first step in his method is "to know these books," namely the books of the entire Catholic canon, Old and New Testament, which he has enumerated in the chapter immediately preceding. Augustine means for his students really to *know* the text: the goal is memorization. "Although we may not yet understand them, nevertheless, by reading them we can either memorize them or become somewhat acquainted with them."[120] As is clear from what follows, Augustine intends that his students be able to move, in their own minds, from passage to passage with great ease, hearing the verbal echoes of one text in another and thereby able to have almost a concordance of texts in their memory. In Chapter 14 of Book II, Augustine says that students should keep a running list of unknown words in their minds so that when they meet the word again, in another place, the new context might give them its meaning. That Augustine worked this way himself is clear. His own expositions on the psalms, to cite only one example, often read as if he were working from a modern concordance; an important word in one text is explained by its context in other passages. Later exegetes, especially within the monastic tradition but including Dhuoda, adopted the same hermeneutic and often demonstrate the same facility.

Once the biblical texts are *known* in this manner, Augustine proposes two simple rules for understanding them. The student begins with those texts which are more easily understood, those which contain "rules, governing either life or belief;"[121] presumably these are either more obvious in the text itself and/or are understood because they are central to Christian life and have been explained by the church. These rules, which include both credal formulae and moral codes, must be "studied more

---

[120] p. 71.

[121] p. 71.

intelligently and more attentively" because such study leads to "discernment."[122] The word "discernment" is an important one; it describes a quality of mind that is at once intellectual and practical. Discernment is a way of knowing that results from both an academic study and the attempt to practice what is studied. It is another indication that Augustine's method is meant for practical theology.

When discernment is gained, the student can turn to the more obscure passages of Scripture. Now a "certain intimacy with the language of the Holy Scriptures" will enable her to understand obscure passages more easily and the wisdom achieved from studying and practicing the rules of faith and life will "remove the uncertainty from doubtful passages."[123] Again Augustine notes that in this total process of appropriating the Scriptures, the memory is crucial. The method of letting one piece of scriptural text explain the meaning of another will not work at all well if the texts themselves have not been committed to memory.[124] This method of Augustine, simple but intensive, found expression in the *lectio divina* of the monastic world and resulted in the tradition of the great monastic treatises leading through the twelfth-century Cistercians directly to scholastics such as Bonaventure. As Robert E. McNally notes, "the result of long years of this monastic prayer was a total interior saturation with the words and ideas of Scripture. The *lectio divina* was the foundation and the beginning of all monastic *meditatio* and *contemplatio*, just as at a later date it would

---

[122] pp. 71–72.

[123] p. 72.

[124] At the same time, reliance on memory often means that texts are paraphrased rather than quoted directly. This often engages modern readers in the difficult task of tracing biblical *echoes* rather than explicit citations in medieval texts.

be the foundation and beginning of all *quaestio* and *disputatio*."[125]
It is within this methodological tradition that the work of Dhuoda
lies.

Early Exegetical History of the Story

Dhuoda's method is, then, primarily the *lectio divina* of the
monastic tradition. That tradition, however, did not expect the
student of Scripture to read the biblical texts unaided. Consulting
classical commentaries and homilies ensured that the monastic
student both understood the text and interpreted it in harmony with
orthodox faith. Therefore, Dhuoda's interpretation of the story of
the Syro-Phoenician woman will be best understood against the
background of its exegetical history. Though the exegesis of
Origen lies outside the Latin Western tradition most accessible to
Dhuoda, Origen did influence that tradition greatly because of
Jerome's extensive use of his work. Therefore his exegesis makes
an appropriate starting-point for the exegetical history of the story
of the Syro-Phoenician woman. In his *Commentary on Matthew*,[126]
Origen begins with the allegorical meaning of the geography of the
story. He then raises the questions which will receive the attention
of later commentators: who does the woman represent, and what is
the meaning of the loaves, the crumbs, the dogs and the children?
He also looks for the parallel, in his own concrete situation, to the
antithesis set up in the original story between the children and the
dogs. This is the general outline which later commentators will
follow.

Origen's exegesis of this story is unified by his conviction that
rationality, the degree to which a human being is dominated by
logos, is determinative in the process of salvation. Origen first

---

[125] *The Bible in the Early Middle Ages* (Atlanta, GA: Scholars Press Reprint,
1985), 9.

[126] Trans. by John Patrick in *ANF* 10 (Grand Rapids, MI: Eerdmans Publishing
Co, 1975), 444–447.

distinguishes between Jerusalem/Israel, Canaan and "the borders." The borders are the transitional places between Israel (the land of faith and virtue) and Tyre and Sidon (the land of gentiles, evil powers, wickedness and passions). For Origen, the bread refers to the Words of Jesus and the relative quantities of bread (loaves and crumbs) are distributed according to the rational capacity of those who receive the bread of life. "And perhaps, also, of the words of Jesus there are some loaves which it is possible to give to the more rational, as to children only; and other words, as it were, crumbs from the great house and table of the well-born and the masters, which may be used by some souls, like the dogs" (446–7). The "children" in the story are the rational souls, the Israelites whom Origen describes as "a lost race of souls *possessed of clear vision.*"[127] When the Jews turn away from God, they are replaced by others, who are able to come to faith because they are essentially rational persons.   In Origen's understanding, ". . . it is pre-eminently the work of the Word to save the more intelligent, for these are more akin to Him than those who are duller" (446). The dogs, then, are the irrational and passionate, because "wickedness, and mad fury in wanton discourses and shamelessness, contribute to the giving of a man the name of dog. . ." (447).

Within this carefully constructed allegorical interpretation, the Syro-Phoenician woman is a type, not precisely of the church, but of those who "pass over" from the irrationality and brutishness of sin to virtue through the power of faith. In Origen's understanding of the virtues, faith makes one more rational as well as a child of God. For Origen, then, the antithesis of the story consists in an exchange of conditions between those who first receive faith and those to whom it is given later, an exchange which, in Origen's view, is against right reason (though not beyond the power of

---

[127] Emphasis mine. Origen's ambiguity toward the Jews is apparent here. He carefully distinguishes the Israel in the flesh from the Israel of the Spirit (e.g., *De principiis* IV, I, 22); yet his appreciation of the Jews as the chosen of God and as a race of religious and reasonable culture, to whom he was indebted for his own learning, is never lost.

Jesus).   The coming-to-faith of the Syro-Phoenician Woman therefore upsets the rational order of things. The intellectual elitism present in this bit of commentary is central to Origen's understanding of the allegorical method itself, in which the higher reaches of scriptural understanding are reserved for those who follow a path defined by intellectual achievement as well as moral discipline. In Origen's framework, this path was virtually closed to woman by her naturally limited capacity for rationality. Ironic, therefore, is his interpretation of the Syro-Phoenician woman as a symbol of faith, and it intensifies the way in which, for him, faith overturns the rational and natural order of reality.

   After Origen, there is not an extensive commentary tradition on the pericope of the Syro-Phoenician woman, probably because it found no place in the major liturgical cycles. But there is one particular historical trajectory against which it is reasonable to examine Dhuoda's use of the story. That trajectory is created by Jerome's *Commentary on Matthew* and Bede's *Commentary on Mark*. Jerome's influence on later exegesis is too obvious to need comment here. He was one of the writers most well represented in the libraries of the Carolingians as analyzed by McKitterick and Riché.   His commentary on Matthew is cited in the Marcan commentary by Bede whose exegetical and historical works are also significantly represented in the library catalogs and other documentary evidence of the period.   Selections from Bede's exegetical material turn up frequently in the Carolingian homiliaries.[128] In the seminal Carolingian homiliary compiled by

---

[128] Almost all the scholars in the field, beginning with Smalley, note Bede's extensive influence on later medieval continental exegesis. As Smalley notes, "Bede affected medieval scholarship in two ways; he made a wide range of authors readily accessible and he set an example of eager curiosity in their use. He had St. Jerome's ardour for *lectio divina* disciplined by the Benedictine rule" (36). Also see, inter alia, Henri Barre, "L'Homiliare Carolingien de Mondsee," *RB* 71 (1961): 75; Jean LeClercq, "Le IIIe libre de Homelies de Bede le Venerable," *RecTh* 14 (1947): 211–218; M. L. W. Laistner, "A Ninth Century Commentator on the Gospel According to Matthew," *Harvard Theological Review* 20 (1927): 131.

Paul the Deacon for Charlemagne, there are thirty-four homilies taken from Bede's *Homilies on the Gospels*; additional selections, taken from Bede's commentaries, make his contributions almost one-quarter of Paul's total work.[129] The homily that Smaragdus gives for the story of the Syro-Phoenician woman is composed almost entirely of connected passages from Jerome and Bede and the later Homiliary of Aelfric is almost entirely dependent on Bede.[130] Therefore, the commentaries of Jerome and Bede seem to make up an identifiable line of the Latin tradition to which Dhuoda could reasonably have had access and whose interpretations she might well have heard even if she did not consult their texts. In the discussion which follows, special attention will be paid to whether and how Jerome, Bede and Dhuoda assign a specific allegorical meaning to the various elements of the narrative; what particular elements of the story call for the most detailed exposition on the part of each author; and how the central antithesis of the original story is analyzed in the light of the historical context of the writer.

Jerome

The earliest Latin development of the story of the Syro-Phoenician woman belongs, of course, to Jerome's *Commentary on Matthew*.[131] The commentary was written in 398 at the request of a rather troublesome friend, Eusebius of Cremona; it was a parting-gift as he set sail for Rome. Like Origen before him, Jerome gives a carefully detailed allegorical interpretation to the main details of the gospel story: the geography, the woman and

---

[129] Martin, "Introduction," xiv.

[130] Cyril L. Smetana, "Aelfric and the Early Medieval Homiliary," *Traditio* 15 (1959): 197.

[131] Ed. Emile Bonnard, *SC*, Vol 242 and 243 (Paris: Editions du Cerf, 1977, 1978). See Appendix Two for an English translation of Jerome's commentary on this gospel.

her daughter, the crumbs and, finally, the children and the dogs. For Jerome, Tyre and Sidon represent the errors of pagan lands, and the woman's action of leaving her borders represents both a change of place and an inner change of heart. In these contextual details, Jerome stays close to the historical level of the text, though he extends it to a more universal meaning. The woman is the church in whom Jerome finds the three specific qualities of faith, patience and humility, but the daughter, though Jerome explicitly honors her with the title "daughter of the church," represents for him idolaters "who are ignorant of the Creator and therefore adore stone images" (II, 15, 146).[132]

The bread which is the source of contention between the dogs and the children receives little attention in Jerome's commentary. He merely notes of the crumbs that, though they are only humble pieces, through each the whole is shared, a vague and veiled reference to the Eucharistic theology of the early church. The image of the dogs, however, seems to exercise Jerome's imagination. They are "ethnici," members of alien cultures and tribes, indeed barbarians, who are caught up in idolatrous religions in which their eating of blood and dead flesh fills them with rage. The reference is probably to the animal sacrifices of pagans with, perhaps, an implied contrast to the Eucharistic sacrifices of the Christians. Though it would be twelve years before the sack of Rome which Jerome mourned so eloquently in his letters, by 395 the Visigoths under Alaric had already devastated much of Macedonia and Greece and threatened Constantinople.[133] As Kelly notes, these earlier incursions of the "barbarians" much occupied Jerome's mind and filtered into his correspondence in the years just before his writing of this commentary; he cites specifically Letter #60, which Jerome wrote to Heliodorus on the death of his nephew

---

[132] In Jerome's use of allegory here, we see one of the dangers of the method. The various meanings assigned to the daughter are not quite coherent.

[133] J. N. D. Kelly, *Jerome: His Life, Writings and Controversies* (San Francisco: Harper and Row, 1975), 295.

Nepotian in 396.[134] The image of the dog-like, blood-thirsty "ethnici" is therefore probably colored by Jerome's reflections on the social and political crisis unfolding around him.

The part of the story which calls forth Jerome's most detailed exposition is the response of Jesus to the woman's request (v. 23 in Matt). Jerome is concerned here to explain the human and historical meaning of the actions and intentions of Jesus which, precisely on a historical level, could be seen as inappropriate.[135] Perhaps the key to understanding Jerome's interpretation of Jesus' motivations lies in the emphasis he places on the atmosphere of calumny which he sees surrounding the ministry of Jesus. Jerome's emphasis on "calumny" in this commentary is provocative. Though a list of human vices comes shortly before the story of the Syro-Phoenician woman (both in Matt and Mk) in which Jesus names false accusation (Gk: *pseudomarturiai)* along with murder, fornication and blasphemy as those things which proceed from the human heart and defile the human person, the Vulgate does not use the Latin *calumnia* here whereas Jerome, in the commentary, repeats it twice. Knowing how much Jerome felt that he was repeatedly the victim of the kind of misrepresentation and malicious persecution that *calumnia* signifies, we are tempted to see in his emphasis a subtle identification of himself with Jesus. Jesus leaves familiar country to avoid the kind of malicious persecution that Jerome perceived himself to have received in Rome before leaving for the deserts of Asia Minor. He begins his commentary on this pericope by noting that Jesus has gone over to Tyre and Sidon precisely to get away from scribes and pharisees who were calumniating him (21, 37–38).

---

[134] p. 215.

[135] For a modern reading of the story which uses the shocking elements of Jesus' behavior, understood historically, as the hermeneutical key to the passage, see Sharon Ringe, "A Gentile Woman's Story," L. M. Russell (ed.), *Feminist Interpretation of the Bible* (Oxford: Blackwell, 1985).

In attempting to explain Jesus' response to the Syro-Phoenician woman he again refers to the scribes and pharisees by contrasting Jesus' attitude to theirs: his silence does not come from pharisaical pride nor scribal contempt but from a need for consistency so that those enemies will find no grounds for calumny (23, 149–155). Therefore, Jesus first "answers not a word" to the woman in order to be faithful to his own earlier injunction (Matt 10:5) that the newly-named Apostles not go into pagan territories. Then, when Jesus does respond, harshly, with the logion about the dogs not worthy of the children's bread (v. 24), Jerome posits that Jesus is merely being careful to observe the proper order of the plan of God. He must be concerned first about the lost sheep of Israel, so that when they reject him (Jerome implies that Jesus knows that they will), he will be justified in turning his attention to the Gentiles. This care will forestall the objections of those who are looking for reasons to condemn him. Jerome says that the divine purpose to save the Gentiles is eternal; yet the human proprieties must be observed and the chosen people must be given their full and fair opportunity first.

In this context Jerome attempts to explain the response of the Apostles to the woman's presence and request. He suggests that the Apostles do not know the temporal sequence laid out for the eternal mystery of salvation; the gift of full salvation for the Gentiles will come only with the death and resurrection of Jesus. The Apostles, therefore, are not yet moved by evangelical compassion and are burdened by her harassment. Jesus takes the opportunity, therefore, as a good teacher will, to explain to his Apostles the parable of the lost sheep, by speaking here of the "lost sheep of Israel." In addition to observing his own careful timing of the divine plan, Jesus prepares the Apostles for the gentile mission which will come later by using this incident to illuminate the foundational parable of the lost sheep. The scholar and teacher in Jerome obviously found a point of commonality with the Matthean portrait of Jesus as teacher; he attributes to Jesus his own magisterial method of explaining in one place what he has said in another.

Jerome subtly reinforces his exoneration of Jesus by ignoring Jesus' reference to the woman as a "dog." In his exposition of v. 24, he analyzes Jesus' intentions, not his language. He attributes the use of the term dog to the woman herself, an expression of her humility. He notes that she uses the term for young dog or puppy, *catellus* rather than *canis*, and he interprets the word as simply young dog or puppy.[136] Jerome dramatizes the woman's inner feelings; he embellishes her responses with additional, self-deprecating words as if he would drive home his message. Her principal virtue is the humility by which she acknowledges her lowly status and her contentedness with "mere crumbs" (through which, however, she may receive the "greatness" of the whole bread). At the same time, Jerome has changed her word for the host from "master" to "father": the reward of such humility is increased intimacy. In keeping with his fundamental understanding of the Syro-Phoenician woman as an image of the church, he has, with a few sure strokes, developed her character and has even changed her words so that she is, indeed, a model of the faith, patience, and humility he has attributed to her.

The original gospel story leads up to the implied antithesis between the dogs and the children. The children are originally favored by the bread which the master supplies. The dogs succeed in acquiring that bread through their faith, which Jesus praises in his closing word. Jerome calls this a marvelous reversal in the order of things (but not a reversal of the *rational* order as in Origen) signified by the exchange of names. His antithesis is that the children of Israel become dogs (he quotes Phil 3:2) while the gentiles acquire faith. He does not complete the chiasmus and leaves the idea that the gentiles become children merely implied, as did the original text. In fact, he does not go beyond the original

---

[136] G. H. R. Horsley, *New Documents Illustrating Early Christianity*, indicates that fourth century usage of this word most often indicated affection rather than the size or age of the dog (Macquarrie University: The Ancient History Documentary Research Centre, 1987), 157–158. Jerome adheres to the literal meaning.

gospel understanding of the dogs and children (the earlier interpretation of the dogs as idolaters is not repeated here) and makes no attempt to find parallels in any but the most general contemporary situation: that the church has become, in Jerome's time, entirely a gentile institution.

Bede

The exegetical work of Bede on this passage is found in his commentary on the gospel of Mark[137] and in Homily 1.22 in his *Homilies on the Gospels.*[138] Both of these works were written sometime after 716, the commentary at the request of Bishop Acca and many of his monastic companions.[139] The homilies would have been preached or, possibly, written for private or public devotional reading.   In the analysis which follows, I shall follow the development of Bede's ideas in the commentary, which is more carefully structured than the homily and from which the homily diverges only slightly.[140]

Because he is commenting on the Marcan parallel, Bede begins with an exposition of Mark's own introductory verse, a reference to the secrecy about which Mark's Jesus is consistently concerned; he follows Jerome in investigating the motivation of Jesus. He writes that Jesus went from Israel to Tyre and Sidon so that he might, through the faith of the woman, put in clear light the lack of faith of the scribes and pharisees.   The structure of Bede's

---

[137] *In Marci Evangelium Exposito*, ed. D. Hurst, *CC* 120 (Turnholt: Brepols, 1960), 523–525.

[138] *CC* 122.

[139] C. E. Whiting, "The Life of the Venerable Bede," in A. Hamilton Thompson (ed), *Bede: His Life, Times, and Writings* (New York: Russell and Russell, 1966), 21.

[140] For an English translation of Bede's commentary on this pericope, see Appendix Three.

exegetical efforts here is illuminating. He divides his commentary on the pericope into two parts and, since he explicitly indicates that the second part is his "mystical" interpretation of the story, we must assume that in the first part he is interpreting its historical meaning. In this part he follows Jerome closely, quoting him at some length (though with a striking omission). In his interpretation, Bede concentrates on the meaning of the woman, her journey and the dogs. Bede says explicitly that the woman is a "type" of the church. But in the light of his own historical situation he nuances her typological significance in a way that brings it closer both to the historical meaning of the original text and to his own concrete circumstances. She is the church gathered from the nations ("ecclesiam designat de gentibus collectam," 1368-69).[141] Like Jerome, he sees particular importance in her action of passing over out of her borders. This makes her not only "ecclesia" but also "evangelista" who leaves her own land in order to save her own people (symbolized by her daughter—a meaning closer to the text than Jerome's understanding of "idolaters"). One thinks immediately of the closing book of his *Historia Ecclesiastica Gentis Anglorum* in which he demonstrates the maturity of the English church by their sending of missionaries to the people of Saxony in Europe to whom they were related.

This journey is obviously a point of great importance to Bede and he gives it further elaboration by playing on the related ideas embodied in the words "errare" and "ingredior." Those who wander aimlessly ("errare") and are therefore in error must be the object of the prayer and missionary journey of those who first have the courage to leave their previous homes ("mansiones") of faithlessness and enter into ("ingredior") the true house of God, the

---

[141] In the homily, Bede repeats this phrase. There, however, he also describes this woman as having the virtues described by revelation, though not the revelation itself because she is a Gentile (215 of the English translation). It is a provocative suggestion about the possibility of moral righteousness in those outside the faith.

church (1372–77).[142] Again, this reflects the historical situations about which Bede wrote in his history. Perhaps he is even thinking specifically about such women as Bertha, Queen of Kent, who left her Christian Gaul to marry Ethelbert and whose prayerful Christian presence anticipated and prepared the ground for the missionary activity of Augustine. In any event, he resolves the question of the Jews by a brief summary of Jerome's thought, calling them habitually esteemed Sons of God who deserve to receive the food of life (a metonymy for salvation) before it is distributed to the nations. There is no hint here of any rejection or exclusion of the Jews. Having followed the general movement of Jerome's commentary, Bede now quotes him at some length (1386-97), writing into his text Jerome's extended allegory on the faith, patience and humility of the church as exemplified by the Syro-Phoenician woman. Significantly, however, Bede omits the sentence in which Jerome identifies the dogs as heathens *(ethnici)* who practice idolatrous blood sacrifices and he proceeds to Jerome's statement of the glorious paradox by which the dogs and children exchange places. Would the reference to the *"ethnici"* as dogs have been too close to a negative reflection on his own countrymen? Certainly Bede does so identify them in his later, "mystical" interpretation. "We are those dogs," says Bede, "and we have been converted from the barking of blasphemous contradiction" (1397–98). But there, the use of the first-person plural pronoun and the affectionate tone remove much of the sting in the label of dog while Jerome's sentence would here have, perhaps, been genuinely offensive. This explanation is consonant with Bede's explanation of Christ's reference to the "lost sheep."

---

[142] One thinks of Augustine's frequent use of the image of the creature of God as someone on a journey who frequently wanders ("errare") into the land of unlikeness (sin), but is never without hope of return; who can find inns of refreshment along the way, but never a permanent home in this changing world. Augustine was, of course, one of Bede's major sources as he was one of Dhuoda's favorites.

At this point Jerome had brought in the parable of the lost sheep, saying that Jesus the Teacher wishes to explain the meaning of the parable by his word about the "lost sheep of the house of Israel."[143] Bede follows his lead, but quotes instead another sheep-saying, that of Jn 10:16. For Bede, this citation reveals that those *who have been considered* dogs are, in reality, simply other sheep, not yet of the fold. Later in his commentary he will point out that these dogs/sheep were, prior to their conversion, *looked upon* with contempt ("qui erant despecti in gentibus," 1410), but he seems to imply that they were never truly other than sheep whose time had not yet come. This whole line of argumentation seems designed to nuance the identification of the dogs with the members of the English nation. Bede makes the identification, but cites and interprets other verses to show the ultimate Christian destiny of the English in the merciful plan of God. The antithesis, even the distinction, between the dogs and the children has virtually disappeared.

Bede uses Jerome with great care and discrimination; the earlier text has been carefully edited to illustrate the situation of the Germanic tribes of England, latecomers as they are to the story of salvation, and to reassure rather than denigrate those who have come relatively recently into the church. He modifies Jerome precisely in terms of his own historical situation, demonstrating, perhaps, that for him "historical interpretation" of the biblical text means that the history of the narrative was interpreted in the light of one's own history.

---

[143] In his homily on this pericope, Bede includes something of Jerome's commentary that he does not include here. He explores, as Jerome did, the question of why Jesus responds so harshly to the woman, asking, however, why Jesus kept the woman waiting. He gives three reasons: 1) to demonstrate her patience; 2) to teach mercy to the Apostles; 3) to give no occasion to the Jews for finding fault with his teaching Gentiles. Like Jerome, he explains that Jesus wishes to restrict his own ministry to Jews, while teaching the Apostles that they will be sent to the Gentiles. See *Bede the Venerable: Homilies on the Gospels*, 216.

All of this seems to have been Bede's understanding of the *historical* meaning of the text, because he introduces the rest of his commentary on this passage with an explicit statement that he is moving to the mystical meaning (1400–1402).[144] In this section he gives a more detailed explanation of the dogs, the table, and the bread, distinguishing carefully and symbolically between the crumbs and the crust. As he illuminated the meaning of the dogs above by identifying them with the "other sheep" of the Johannine logion, so here he derives the meaning of the various allegorical elements by parallel citations in which the term in question is given its mystical meaning. The table becomes the Holy Scripture (citing Ps 22:5, "You have prepared a table for me in the sight of my enemies") and the crumbs, the inner meaning of those Scriptures (citing Ps 147:14, "The one who made peace within your borders has filled you with the marrow of wheat").[145]

The distinction between dogs and children remains blurred here; Bede speaks of the "crumbs of the children" in line 1405 and in 1409 says that the dogs do not eat the crusts but the crumbs of the children. In fact, Bede has replaced the antithesis between dogs and children with one between the crumbs and the crusts of the bread of life. For him, the crusts refer to the superficial letter of the Scriptures while the crumbs signify the marrow of the spiritual sense. This antithesis does create a new distinction between those under the table, be they dogs or children, who are fed with the bread of life. Here the distinction is not created by whether some are called early or late to the table but by the willingness of all those who are so called to eschew the "crusts" of the bread of life (the

---

[144] "Notandum sane quod mystice loquitur credens ex gentibus mulier quia catelli sub mensa comedunt de micis puerorum."

[145] Even here, where Bede is adverting explicitly to the mystical meaning of the text, the choice of his citations, with its echoes of "enemies" and "peace-making" remind the reader of the long and tumultuous history of the English church which Bede will narrate in the *Historia Ecclesiastica*. There, of course, the creation of peace between the various ethnic nations becomes the sign of genuine conversion and submission to the "reign of God."

"superficial letter of its meaning") and collect the crumbs ("the very marrow of the spiritual sense"). He even hints (as will Dhuoda after him) that the dogs may have the advantage if they seek to make progress in good deeds, attempting to accomplish in their hearts and with their hands all that has been commanded. For Bede, it is moral improvement rather than the eloquence of holy words that is the condition for understanding the mysteries of the word of God. Distinctions are to be made in Bede's church, then, not between orders, nor between ethnic groups, nor yet between those converted first or last, but between those who allow the Scriptures to transform their lives rather than those for whom it remains merely a question of eloquence. For one whose chief joy and life-long task was teaching, this commentary is an eloquent self-revelation.

Bede ends his exposition of this passage with a practical ecclesiological consideration.[146] He sees a justification for infant baptism in the fact that the woman's faith brought about the exorcism of the daughter. So too, he says, can the confession of faith on the part of the parents in baptism free small children from the devil (1419–1423). This ending note reminds us again how specifically Bede wrote for the church of his day as well as how dominant was the role played by the monasteries in the overall structure and life of the English church. Utilizing the earlier Latin tradition, even quoting extensively from Jerome and following his method closely, he re-invigorates that tradition by reinterpreting it within the situation of his own church. Like the scribe praised by Jesus, Bede thereby brings forth from his treasury new things and old.

---

[146] In the homily, Bede's conclusion is more specific to the life of the monks. He ends by allegorizing the figure of the daughter. Not only is she "any soul delivered up to malign spirits" and therefore in need of the prayers of her mother the church; she also designates whatever remains of vice and darkness in the individual Christian. This allows Bede to elaborate on the need for prayer and the qualities which make prayer effective in combatting the on-going power of "the ancient enemy" (219–21).

Dhuoda's Interpretation of the Story of the Syro-Phoenician Woman

Dhuoda of Septimania, as an educated woman of the ninth century, shared with Bede this sense of tradition as a treasury to be mined for the personal, practical needs of life. Throughout her book, she refers to the characters and wisdom of the biblical texts as the norm and inspiration of her life. She continually refers, as well, to the earlier Christian writers and authorities as dependable teachers in the interpretation of the text. Nonetheless, one may legitimately ask whether, in seeking to position the text of Dhuoda within the tradition of Jerome and Bede, one is not stretching the limits of comparison. They were, after all, scientific scholars writing full commentaries, considering each verse of the gospel narrative within the framework of a coherent exposition. Further, in spite of the essentially didactic and pragmatic purposes of the earlier writers, Dhuoda is *using* the story of the Syro-Phoenician woman in a more *explicitly* personal way than Jerome and Bede, even if my understanding of the *implicit* personal references within their work may be allowed to stand. She is interested, really, in only one point: her right to share in the divine wisdom which comes from the Scriptures. Nonetheless she sets up an exposition of the text which, though both limited and modest, is not unlike the earlier works. She sets up a unified allegory similar to Bede's in its focus on the table, the crumbs and the dogs/children. In line with both Bede and Jerome, she accepts the essential antithesis with which the narrative concludes, but re-works it for her own purposes. According to John J. Contreni, one of the critical characteristics of Carolingian exegesis is the consistency with which it is shaped for a particular audience, usually intimately known to the writer.[147] Like her more professional contemporaries,

---

[147] "Carolingian Biblical Studies," Uta-Renate Blumenthal (ed), *Carolingian Essays* (Washington, DC: The Catholic University of America Press, 1983), 71–98.

Dhuoda keeps in mind at all times the particular, even narrow, capabilities of her specific audience. Her very personal appropriation of the text, therefore, is not outside the general development in Carolingian exegesis, although even in comparison with her contemporaries, the degree of her intimate self-revelation is noteworthy.

The text in question comes very early in the *Liber Manualis*. Dhuoda has, in fact, worked into her material very carefully, even tentatively, and there are several "beginnings" to it. After the title, there is a section of some 50 (printed) lines in which she identifies the nature of the book, gives the etymology of its titles (both "Liber" and "Manualis") and describes some of its literary features. Then comes an "Incipit" in which she tells her son William the circumstances of her undertaking the work followed by a long series of epigrammatic verses, the first letter of each of which forms an acrostic which reads: DHUODA DILECTO FILIO WILHELMO SALUTEM LEGE. Then there is a short prologue, introduced again by "Incipit," in which she defends herself for undertaking such a task in spite of her weakness, and elaborates, nonetheless, on the value and importance of this work for William's welfare. Following the Prologue, Dhuoda gives a Preface, in which she relates the details of her marriage, her childbearing and her present situation, isolated from both husband and sons. At length, one arrives at Book I, consisting of five chapters on God, his attributes and relationship to the human community, followed by two chapters on the moral consequences of being in relationship with God. It is as if she were working up the courage to assume the role of biblical commentator and teacher. In this context, the exposition of the story of the Syro-Phoenician woman, which comes early in the first book, becomes a culminating, and even bold, statement of self-justification.

Dhuoda introduces her use of the text by an impassioned and intimate self-revelation. She speaks first of the serious obligation, incumbent upon both her and her son, to seek God, in whom they live and move and have their being. We hear clear echoes of Augustine, *DDC*, Book VI; Dhuoda is the kind of Christian whom

Augustine bids begin a study of the Scripture with the desire to "seek the will of God." This is the core of Christian life for her as well as for Augustine. She then says that she has both studied to the limits of her strength, though she is both "unworthy and frail as a shadow" and she has petitioned God's help *incessantly* that she might know and understand.[148]   By her use of the adverb "indesinenter" to describe her own prayer for understanding, she is already drawing an implicit parallel between herself and the Syro-Phoenician woman who was a model of persistence. She then reiterates that to understand is an absolute necessity for her.[149]   In this we hear the intellectual and spiritual urgency of the Carolingian period take a particular woman's voice.   She acknowledges elsewhere that mystical prayer may supply, for some, the spiritual wisdom that they desire; for her, that wisdom has been hard won, through arduous study.   At the same time, Dhuoda sees such wisdom as God's gift. That is demonstrated here by her exposition of the gospel narrative which follows immediately upon her personal statement.

Her exposition is intended to demonstrate that human unworthiness is not an obstacle to understanding the mysteries of God and to identify what is required to attain that understanding. It is important to remember her intended audience here: because she is writing this for her son, the lesson about what is required to overcome the obstacle to unworthiness is not merely self-justification but a more general truth, as pertinent to a young, newly empowered warrior as to herself. Indeed she has linked them both together in the opening words of the chapter, "You and I must both seek for God, my son."[150]   Appropriately, then, she begins her exposition not with an explanation of the

---

[148] "Certe et ego, quanquam indigna fragilisque ad umbram,eum, ut ualeo, quaero, et eius adiutorium, ut scio et intelligo, et indesinenter peto" (I, 2, 3–6).

[149] "Est etenim mihi ualde per omnia necesse" (I, 2, 6–7).

[150] "Quarendus est Deus, fili, mihi et tibi" (I, 2, 2).

Syro-Phoenician woman (with whom she has just implicitly compared herself), but with an explanation of the meaning of the table, the dogs, and the crumbs of the bread of life.

For Dhuoda, the table is both the altar and, by metonymy, the church itself; she says that to be under the table is to be inside holy church (15–16). From the table fall the crumbs which are, as in Bede, significant of divine wisdom. Dhuoda does not supply a particular meaning for the dogs, though she implies that she is one of them. Just after she describes her own persistent prayer for understanding, she makes her transition into the gospel passage by affirming that, among the dogs under the table, the importunate or aggressive one can succeed in catching valuable crumbs. "For it may sometimes happen that a persistent puppy, under the table of the Lord with the other dogs, can grab and eat the crumbs that fall."[151] But she focuses her attention particularly on the meaning of the bread, the graciousness of God in providing it and the attentiveness and energy of those who receive it. These three points form, for her, an interrelated pattern in the story of the Syro-Phoenician woman which she finds repeated elsewhere in the Scriptures. In her exposition, she uses the Augustinian and monastic exegetical method of using alternate verses from Scripture to illuminate the meaning of a term or reality in the text at hand. In doing this, Dhuoda follows a pattern of citations similar to that of Bede. She clusters several citations (Num 22:28, Lk 24:25 and Ps 118:125) to illustrate God's power to open up the mouth of dumb animals, as well as the human mind, to the understanding of divine things. This idea provokes a comment on God's generosity in preparing a table for those who are attentive and in providing a full and satisfying measure of grain. To elaborate on this, she cites Ps 78:19, "[Can God spread] a table in the wilderness" and Lk 12:42, "a satisfying measure of wheat" (12–14). It is at the same point in the exposition, namely, the explaining of the meaning of the

---

[151] "Nam solet fieri ut aliquotiens importuna catula, sub mensa domini sui, inter catulos alteros, micas cadentes ualeat carpere et mandere" (I, 2, 7–9)

crumbs as the bread of life and the mysteries of Scripture, that Bede also quotes two citations, different from those Dhuoda chooses but to exactly the same point and with identical images; there are some verbal connections as well.

Dhuoda's text	*Bede's text*
qui *parat* fidelibus suis	"*Parasti* in conspectu meo adversus eos qui
"in deserto *mensam*" (Ps 77:19)	tribulant meo *mensam*" (Ps 23:5)
dansque illis "in tempore" necessitatis	"Qui posuit fines tuos pacem et adipe
satietatem "tritici mensuram" (Lk 12:42)	frumentum *satiens* te" (Ps 147:14)

Both Bede and Dhuoda have cited biblical texts to gloss the idea of the table and the bread; they both choose texts which highlight the notion of God setting the table for the chosen ones and of wheat which is plentiful or satisfying. Bede quotes an entire psalm verse in each case, while Dhuoda integrates the pertinent phrases of her two citations into her own sentence. Where Bede's quoted psalm speaks of a table spread "for me," Dhuoda says "for God's faithful." Bede's "in a time of peace" becomes, in Dhuoda, a "time of necessity." The verbal echoes are slight, to be sure (though Dhuoda does add a form of the verb *satio*, "to fill," which is in Bede and not in her citation). But the similarity of structure in images and thought, occurring as it does in these two passages on the same pericope, suggests something more than coincidence, though less than textual dependence.

In her treatment of the gospel story, Dhuoda makes no mention whatever of the daughter, somewhat surprising in that she is writing for her own progeny. She has completely identified the children with the dogs and placed herself (and by implication, her son) among them, as did Bede; but she does not thereby ignore the antithesis inherent in the original story. Her distinction is between the little dogs who are farther away from, but still under, the table and those who are near. She identifies these two distinct groups as herself and the priests. "At least I may be under his table, that is to say, inside holy church, able to watch even if from afar the small dogs there (that is, the ministers of his holy altars). And under that table I can collect crumbs of spiritual understanding for you and for me."[152] Like the woman in the story, she is content enough to be a little dog under the table (along with everyone else, including the priests) so long as she can attain her own purpose. There she can, by importunate behavior, obtain wisdom for her son as well as for herself, just as the woman's intervention and importunate prayer achieved the exorcism of her daughter.

For Bede, there is no distinction to be made among the dogs under the table, except for the different internal attitudes which each may bring to the study of the word of God. Dhuoda does advert to the distinction created by a particular clerical class, but only to deny that it conveys any special prerogative other than that of being closer to the source.[153] On a literal level, this refers to the liturgical presence of the clergy at the altar and lectern; metaphorically they were also closer to the riches of the church in terms of opportunities for learning. In her exposition, however, the prerogative is minimized by the pertinacity of lay people like herself who pursue divine wisdom with avidity.[154]

---

[152] ". . . psaltim ut sub mensam illius, infra sanctam uidelicet ecclesiam, possim procul conspicere catulos, hoc est sanctis altaribus ministros, et de micis intellectu spirituali mihi et tibi. . . " (I, 2, 15–18).

[153] Dhuoda dedicates Book III, Chap 11 to a more detailed discourse on priests. There she notes their specific duties and privileges, including that of standing closest to the altar. She praises holy priests and warns William not to judge the less holy too harshly. He should give respect to all, but seek counsel only from those who are noteworthy in learning and virtue. Her assessment is gently expressed but filled with worldly realism.

[154] McKitterick has found the opposite emphasis to be more characteristic of the period. "According to the homily [of Rhabanus Maurus] for Sexagesima Sunday the people were obliged to listen in fitting silence to the priest's words, and the layman is without a doubt placed in a position of inferiority to the priest, for he

Whereas Jerome ends his commentary on this passage with his teaching on how Jews and Gentiles have, by his own day, exchanged places in the favor of the Lord, a theological point, and Bede ends with a bit of teaching on a practical and pastoral church problem, Dhuoda ends her exposition with an extended doxology to the eternal God who remains ever what God has always been, the giver of wisdom. Like all good *lectio divina*, Dhuoda's reading of the Scripture brings her to prayer that flows from her reading of the text in the context of her own immediate life-situation. The prayer expresses both a legitimate understanding of the text and the personal needs of the reader. Dhuoda's text is, I believe, an early sample of what is generally called "monastic theology" but which may well be simply the "practical theology" of the early middle ages. The fruit of meditation, this theology is expressed according to liturgical models where the readings, especially of narrative and prophetic books, were interspersed with responsorial verses which echoed and clarified their themes. Dhuoda's work illustrates the way in which early exegetical theology was available (even though with difficulty) to the laity who were able to forge from it a coherent and meaningful framework for interpreting their own lives. If some find early medieval exegesis derivative, the text of Dhuoda (as well as that of Bede) suggests that what was derived was significantly reworked to new and practical uses.

---

can only listen to the Word and carry out its requirements" (*The Frankish Church*, 109). In contrast, Dhuoda insists that she can understand and teach the Word.

Chapter Four

THE BEATITUDES AND THE MORAL LIFE OF THE CHRISTIAN[155]

A t the heart of Dhuoda's *Liber Manualis* is her exposition of the moral life of the Christian programmatically developed for a young man who is expected to take his place as a magnate of the Carolingian empire. The controlling purpose of the book is, as we have seen, her desire to educate William (and his infant brother) in her absence, as she would have done had she been able to live out her maternal vocation in a time of peace. Accordingly, after three chapters in which she writes of God, the theological virtues, prayer and William's place in the social hierarchy (his duties toward his father, princes, his superiors, equals and inferiors), Dhuoda proposes a scheme for his total moral development (Chaps. IV through VI).[157] To construct her program, Dhuoda brings together two strands of traditional material. The overall flow of her text (in Books IV to VI) follows the "catalog of vices" or *psychomachia* genre. Morton W. Bloomfield traces the history of this tradition in *The Seven Deadly Sins*.[158] Into this frame, Dhuoda inserts an interpretation of the gifts of the Holy Spirit and the beatitudes as the constitutive elements of moral development. Here she follows closely a tradition developed by Augustine. In contrast with the preceding chapter in which we see Dhuoda interacting directly with

---

[155] A brief, early version of this chapter was published in *Mystics Quarterly* 18, 1 (March, 1992): 6–15

[156] See Appendix Four for an outline of her scheme.

[157] (Michigan: State College Press, 1952).

a specific biblical text (though not outside of the framework provided by inherited tradition), in her interpretation of the beatitudes and gifts of the Holy Spirit, she is more consciously working with a large body of traditional material already significantly formalized. She is forced to consider not just the meaning of a particular word or phrase as bequeathed to her by the earlier exegetical tradition. She must now consider an entire theological structure that has been built upon an exegetical base and reworked by previous authors. In both cases, she is working within a traditional framework; in both, she is creatively selecting and editing; in both, she is doing work similar to that done by more professional contemporaries. But they are different tasks, exegetically and theologically, and her work on the beatitudes allows us to consider her wider range of theological skills. To understand Dhuoda's work, both as representative of traditional exegesis in the Carolingian period and as an individual, creative contribution, we must see her work in the context of the catalog tradition as well as of Augustine's analysis.

Dhuoda's Use of the Catalog Tradition of Virtues and Vices

Book IV of the *Liber Manualis* begins with an explanation of the general principle that to arrive at human perfection, the Christian must practice the virtues that are opposed to the major vices, a principle she repeats at regular intervals in her text, almost like a refrain. This is precisely the principle on which the *psychomachia* tradition is based. Dhuoda then proceeds to a discussion of envy and pride, vices which she selects from the tradition as of particular pertinence to William. At various points in her analysis of the beatitudes, she inserts analyses of lust, anger and pride and elaborates upon the virtues of patience and generosity (which she considers the best general weapons in the war against all the vices). Short, annotated lists of various other tribulations and temptations (including the ancient monastic vice of sadness) are included near the end, interrupting in fact the framework she constructs of the gifts of the Holy Spirit and the beatitudes.[158] This is, if you will, her description of the war of the virtues and vices and her catalog of the same. In terms of the catalog tradition of moral instruction Dhuoda is generally in line with what Bloomfield calls the monastic line (from Cassian through Gregory the Great to Alcuin).[159] She uses that tradition with great discernment, selecting those virtues and vices which are of greatest importance in William's life and illustrating them from her own store of experience. She follows the general outline of the monastic authors which was, in any case, commonplace by her day, but discusses only a few of the vices in the traditional catalog. If we compare her "list" to those of Cassian, Gregory and Alcuin, we note that she puts envy at its head (against all three) and discusses pride twice.[160] She has her chief reader, William, in mind throughout and deals with the vices which she believes the greatest threat to his spiritual welfare; for these, she gives lively and personal examples. It is in her re-working of the traditional list, but especially in her use of

---

[158] The seams between the various kinds of material she uses are clearly, even awkwardly, evident. She does not blend, but creates a patchwork.

[159] Rosamund McKitterick, *The Frankish Church and the Carolingian Reforms, 789-895* (London: Royal Historical Society, 1977) notes the way in which Alcuin and Gregory represent the catalog tradition. She says of Alcuin's *Concerning Virtues and Vices* that, in it, he was "more concerned with Wido the man and his place in a Christian society than with Wido the Count for it is precisely his committal preoccupations which had distracted Wido to such an extent that he asked Alcuin, according to the preface, to write him some sort of guide for his private morality." McKitterick says that "it is difficult to pinpoint at what stage the private morality so desired by the leaders of society becomes directed towards the good of society as a whole. . ." (168). Dhuoda's text seems to reflect a private morality considered essentially, if not exclusively, within the context of the common good.

[160] Bloomfield, 69–81. Alcuin also rearranges the list rather freely and has two series of treatments in the *DVV* (so that there is a double discussion of major vices), but he is somewhat more inclusive of the whole traditional array of vices/virtues than Dhuoda is.

concrete examples from the aristocratic and militaristic world she shares with William, that we see her personal and creative contribution to the catalog tradition.

In her discussion of three particular vices, namely, envy, lust and anger, she tailors her admonitions to the needs of her young son and fleshes out her moral injunctions with examples that stress the social implications of these vices. For her, their particular danger lies in the way in which they erode or destroy the social relationships which were the foundation of society and the condition of its peace. In her analysis of envy (Book IV, 1), for example, she follows the general thought of Alcuin (*DVV* XXII),[161] even citing *Wisd* 2:24 as he does. But, for her, the vice of envy leads to a consideration of the importance of avoiding evil companions. She quotes Prudence in *Cathemerimon* to describe the demon of envy as a twisted serpent that takes on a myriad of forms[162] and reminds William that envy is the vice of those who are small-minded, those who seek a greatness which they do not have by reason of birth and virtue. Such a vice is not for William, whose parentage has conferred on him nobility and who, she hopes, will also acquire the spiritual nobility of virtue by engaging in a spirited war against the vices. She speaks of the continual vigilance that William must exercise if he would avoid the contamination of evil companions and illustrates this with an example from nature about the dove who, when he comes to drink the limpid stream of truth, watches carefully for hawks and other raptors.[163] She hints that the decline of the family fortunes is to be attributed to these evil

---

[161] *De Virtutibus et Vitiis, PL* 101, 613–38.

[162] "Ille etenim milleformis daemonum tortuosusque serpens" (IV, 1, 25–26).

[163] Bloomfield, 79, points to a tradition of using animal examples in moral instruction. According to his analysis of the tradition, Dhuoda seems to follow the example of Chrysostom in simply using examples from the world of animals; she does not, like Aldhelm of Malmesbury (d. 709) identify vices with specific animals.

companions; they still surround both Dhuoda and William, seeking how they may possess their property and position.

Again, when she discusses the vices of lust and anger, she sees them as vices which particularly pollute human and societal relationships. If her suggested strategies for opposing lust are traditional—fight, pray and remember the example of biblical figures known for their chastity—her descriptions of the real dangers lust poses ring with vivid concreteness and practical realism. Prostitutes are a serious danger because, through them, "you fall under the sword and into the hands of your enemies."[164] The sexually seductive spy was obviously a commonplace of war in Dhuoda's time, as always. Though she quotes Alcuin on chastity as "an angelic life" (*DVV* 18) and Paul on fornication as a sin against one's own body (1 Cor 6:18), Dhuoda's emphasis is on the social destructiveness of lust and fornication: she mentions, as mentors of chastity, the examples of Joseph and Potiphar's wife and Daniel defending the innocence of Susanna (Gen 39:1–23 and Daniel 13).

Appropriately, therefore, she also develops the notion of the beauty of chastity in marriage, lest William think that the words of the traditional masters are an exhortation only for monks and nuns.[165]   A *catena* of verses on the importance of the eyes in chastity opens out into a colorful picture of the lustful person whose eyes turn his head here and there in desire; nevertheless, she points out that chastity is an interior virtue, as well as a communal or societal one. It is described, as she says in anticipation of her later discussion of the beatitudes, by the eighth beatitude: through chastity one enters into the company of the just with its corporate reward, the heavenly banquet. Dhuoda makes a point of the plural verbs in Matt 5:8: the reward of chastity, promised to *many*, is to

---

[164] ". . . facient te cadere in gladio et manus inimicorum tuorum. . ." (IV, 6, 18–19).

[165] IV, 6, 54–59.

join the *company* of other good people. Her description of chastity is not that made specific to a monastic model of perfection; it is a virtue which is an essential part of the fabric of the kingdom of God here on earth and the condition of participation in that kingdom hereafter, essentially a social reality on both planes.

In writing about anger, Dhuoda is even more psychologically realistic. She speaks of anger as a pestilence which will dog William's steps throughout his life. Its particular viciousness, especially in the life of a young warrior like William, is that it pervades all the good actions which a just person initiates and destroys them from within. She warns him that he cannot avoid being moved by anger; he can only refuse to let it overcome and destroy his mind. Against anger, Dhuoda proposes the remedy of patience and alertness, but for her, patience is anything but passivity. Like the other virtues she describes, patience is an element of spiritual warfare; it is the ability to transform anger into energy for the fight against evil and to endure that struggle over a long period of time. She quotes Ps 4:5 here: "be angry but do not sin." The biblical mentor Dhuoda suggests to William, Moses burdened with the governance of six hundred thousand Israelites, is particularly appropriate for her son and adds an ascetic note to the moral advice she is giving. Like Moses, William can expect to be irritated and frustrated by the duties of his state in life; if he would have it said of him, as it was said of Moses, that he was never disturbed by anger, he must follow Moses in *intimacy with God.* According to Dhuoda, Moses was given whatever he asked of God and was marked, especially, by a patient mildness in the midst of all his fighting precisely because he was continually on the alert to encounter God and because he spoke with God "as one person speaks to a friend."[166] Thus, the remedy for anger, an insidious vice that penetrates and corrupts the inner reaches of the soul, is intimacy with God and a vigilant attention to God's

---

[166] ". . . loquebaturque cum Deo, quasi homo cum amico suo, ita ut ex magno magnum mereretur accipere responsum" (IV, 7, 46–48).

presence in that same inner citadel. Dhuoda points to the reward of Moses: he died with his eyesight intact and all his teeth in his mouth, his whole body a vigorous instrument of his soul. Surely this is a humanly appealing reward, especially for one whose strength of body was central to his social position and vocation! But its theological import is significant too: the conquest of the most powerful spiritual enemy results in a perfect integrity of body and soul. As if this were not enough to move an adolescent conscience, Dhuoda adds a final promise of the admiration of society. Everyone, Dhuoda asserts, recognizes that the truly strong person is the one who is patient.

We can see in various chapters of Book IV how Dhuoda both utilizes and modifies the catalog tradition of the virtues and vices, shaping it by her awareness of William's particular circumstances and needs. But she also enlarges the catalog tradition, using it as a general frame into which she inserts another piece of traditional material, that is, a systematic and nuanced treatment of gifts of the Holy Spirit and the eight beatitudes. This will allow her to develop an entire moral program for her adolescent son which is biblically based, in line with the systematic moral tradition available to her and, at the same time, suited particularly to the world and vocation of William. The link between the catalog of vices and the study of the gifts and beatitudes is the theme of warfare.[167] In transitional passages, as she moves back and forth between the two kinds of traditional material, Dhuoda makes the link explicit. Her analysis of the gifts of the Holy Spirit is entitled "Being militant according to the seven-fold gift of the Holy Spirit." The passage is filled with admonitions to "learn," "struggle," "fight" and "work." She speaks repeatedly of William's working and fighting together with his soldier-companions. Again, as a transition between her analysis of the gifts and her thought on the beatitudes, Dhuoda gives a general description of the moral life as a continual battle against vice. For

---

[167] As Bloomfield notes, "The vices against the virtues, against the seven prayers of the paternoster, against the beatitudes, all mingle in a kind of ordered disorder and make part of the mental climate of the Middle Ages" (65).

her, the gifts of the Holy Spirit enable the Christian to "build a strong wall against the encircling waves of other vices"—there is a little word-play in the Latin. Dhuoda envisions a state of siege. The war against vice is never-ending; there is no way to put a definitive end to the assaults of the devil, evil companions and the vicious tendencies of one's own heart. The permanent strategy for Christian life is to continue the assault against successive waves of temptation, launching "arrow for arrow" by "doing good works."[168] The image that holds both passages—and indeed, all of Book IV—together is that of a company of knight-trainees, learning together, not only the arts of warfare, but the benefits and, indeed, necessity of a communal striving for perfection.

This suggests, perhaps, a conscious transformation of the monastic model of perfection. Chapter One of Benedict's Rule describes the two acceptable kinds of monks as those who "wage their war under a rule and an abbot" and those who "have prepared themselves in the fraternal line of battle for the single combat of the hermit."[169] Indeed, the entire Rule is permeated with references to the monastic life as a warfare against the forces of sin, waged in a community of warriors. Dhuoda turns the metaphor back upon itself: the community of those who train for actual war becomes, not just the symbol of, but the actual environment for the spiritual battle against evil. But the gifts and the beatitudes are more than just another example of spiritual warfare for Dhuoda (just as the Benedictine Rule envisioned a greater ideal of perfection than could be imaged in military language). Together they provide a system of programmatic steps by which William can ascend to the greatest spiritual maturity; Dhuoda sees them as constituting the structure of moral development. In this, Dhuoda is following Augustine,

---

[168] "Nunc, auxiliante gratia Sancti Spiritus triformem, ad cetera quae secuntur, quasi sagitam contra sagitam, uitia *morum* emendando, fortem in undis undique obponamus *murum*" (emphasis mine), (IV, 5, 5–8).

[169] Citations are from the translation by Anthony C. Meisel and M. L. del Mastro (Garden City, NY: Doubleday, 1975), 47.

who linked the beatitudes and the gifts in a way that was to become normative for the tradition.[170]

The Augustinian Tradition of the Gifts and the Beatitudes

In their exegesis of Isaiah 11:2–3,[171] the text which speaks of the various gifts of the Spirit, early Christian classical writers had interpreted the text as a description of Christ, the Messiah. Further, they had interpreted the Isaian text as speaking of the fullness of grace of the Holy Spirit rather than as enumerating special gifts. Jerome calls attention to the number of the gifts but makes little of their numbering. It was left to Augustine, with his great love of number symbolism, to stress the importance of the numerical distinction and to see the diverse gifts as hierarchical; he affirms that the Spirit descends from the heights of wisdom to the level of those who fear the Lord so that Christians might, in turn, learn to ascend from fear to wisdom. Augustine virtually ignores the Christological emphasis of earlier commentaries and focuses on the ascetical and anthropological teaching of the Isaian text. In Sermon 147 (*PL* 38: 1524–25) on this text, Augustine briefly delineates the stages of human growth toward perfection and indicates the parallel between those stages and the evangelical teaching of the Matthean beatitudes. He develops this thought at somewhat greater length in his commentary on the sermon on the mount.[172] For Augustine, the

---

[170] J. de Blic, "Pour l'histoire de la theologie des dons," *RAM* 22: 117–79.

[171] See the excellent article by J. Thouzard, "Isaie XI, 2–3 et les sept dons du S. Esprit," *RB* VIII (1899): 249–66.

[172] See Augustine, Sermo 347, *PL* 139, 1524f and *De Sermone Domini in Monte Secundum Matthaeum Libri Duo, PL* 34, 1229–1308. The latter has been translated by John J. Jepson as *The Lord's Sermon on the Mount* for *Ancient Christian Writers* 5 (Westminster, MD: Newman Press, 1956). Citations to the second text will be from the Jepson translation and, for the first, from my own translation.

Matthean sermon on the mount contained the "highest norms of morality" and was "the perfect pattern of the Christian life."[173] The mountain symbolizes the pinnacle of righteousness; the beatitudes epitomize this righteousness and describe the seven stages by which one ascends to it. But for Augustine, the key to understanding these stages lies in the way in which the gifts of the Holy Spirit parallel the beatitudes: only the graces given by the Spirit make possible the human effort detailed by the beatitudes.

Using Ps 111:10, "the fear of the Lord is the beginning of wisdom," as his exegetical key, Augustine is inspired to reverse the order of the gifts as given in Isaiah so that the fear of the Lord marks the initial stage of perfection and wisdom its culmination. He then notes the parallel between the progression of the gifts and that of the beatitudes and his sermon elaborates on the connection between them. To make the scriptural texts fit his schema, he reduces the number of beatitudes to seven, showing that the eighth beatitude "returns, as it were, to the beginning, because it shows and commends what is perfect and complete."[174] This leaves Augustine with two lists of seven stages of human spiritual growth: both begin in lowliness (fear of the Lord and humility) and both end in a state of peace and/or of wisdom, which are, in his understanding, synonymous.

As the first step of the ascent to the mount of perfection, the soul must rid itself of "an inflated spirit" or "high spirits" in order to be filled with the Holy Spirit through appropriate fear of the Lord. This leads almost immediately to meekness and piety, gifts which Augustine translates into a willingness to study the Scriptures with "a godly frame of mind." From this study comes true knowledge which consists in grief for one's own sin. For those who study rightly "come to learn through Scripture with what evils

---

[173] Jepson, 11.

[174] Jepson, 18.

they are held in fetters which aforetime in their ignorance they sought as good things and useful."[175]

Proper mourning for sin and the loss of prized worldly goods lead the soul to crave righteousness and to work for it. At this stage the Christian needs and receives the gift of fortitude, because desire for good is not enough: there must be hard work. The effort demanded to tear oneself away from the delights and responsibilities of the world leads the journeying Christian to discover that he/she is in need of continuous help from God. This leads to the fifth step in the spiritual life, marked by the gift of counsel and the beatitude of mercy. As one seeks more and more help from God in the pursuit of righteousness, one recognizes that such help comes only to those who, in turn, help other weak and vulnerable creatures. We help others in order to be helped by God; we are given counsel in order to transcend the burden of our own efforts. Thence we arrive at understanding; when the heart is purified by works well done, understanding enables the progressing Christian to begin to discern the supreme good. Now, the believer is at the threshold of purity of heart, the ultimate and perfect state for which the human person is destined; that state is the possession of "wisdom itself" in which the "contemplation of the truth, bring[s] peace to the whole [person] and effect[s] a likeness to God."[176]

Augustine's anthropology is foundational to his schema and discernible in his language. The language of stasis and rest abounds; the whole is infused with a sense of order and hierarchy. Even in the early stages of the Christian life, that described for instance in the second beatitude, the rewards promised are static. The "land" which the meek will inherit is "stability," the "state of well being" in which the soul *rests* as in its natural inheritance."[177]

---

[175] Jepson, 19.

[176] Jepson, 18.

[177] Jepson, 14; emphasis mine.

The paradigm of Christian life is the journey from the valley of tears, fear and disordered emotions to the mountain of contemplation, marked by quiescence and interior serenity. The taut way in which Augustine describes the progress from one stage to the next creates the impression that the path of the journey, primarily interior and spiritual, is inexorably fixed. Though Augustine speaks of hard work in the hunger for righteousness, he draws no concrete example of any external work in which the Christian might engage. In spite of the socially active life which Augustine himself led, a life of the episcopal courts and social turmoil, his program for the spiritual life emphasizes the self and individual effort. There is little mention of others: they are there, in the corner of his eye as it were, but the world and worldliness, issues of human power and struggle, of inheritance and battle, are virtually ignored. They are to be abandoned in the search for holiness. The state of wisdom and peace which is the goal of all Christian striving is primarily individual and interior integrity. In the wise, "everything is in order and there is no emotion to rebel against reason, but all things obey the spirit of [the perfect] just as it obeys God."[178] Though in later works, principally in *The City of God*, Augustine will draw up a blueprint of the *res publica* that demonstrates a perfect congruence between individual holiness and the just social order, here the Kingdom of God means the asceticism, grace and spiritual development of the individual Christian.

Dhuoda's Interpretation of the Gifts and Beatitudes

It is quite otherwise when we turn to the text of Dhuoda. The spirit and specific realities of her world permeate the text; they provide her with the metaphors and concrete examples by which she attempts to teach her sons the essential outlines of the Christian life. Though she speaks often and sincerely of the need to pass

---

[178] Jepson, 20.

beyond the transient realities of life and to hunger for what is complete and eternal, though she uses the framework of Augustine and much of the traditional vocabulary of the ascetical tradition, she seems to assume that the real world with all its imperfections and ambiguity is the locus of sanctification and, more, is the stuff of Christian life that must be transformed as the condition of personal holiness. If she knows Augustine's thought, as seems highly likely, she does not follow him in two major aspects: she does not reduce the number of beatitudes in order to complete the numerical parallel with the gifts, nor does she reverse the order of the gifts to make the links between both lists more logical. Rather, the gifts and beatitudes are linked in a *sequential pattern.* In IV, 4, Dhuoda affirms that William's struggle for human growth will be fulfilled by the outpouring of the gifts of the Spirit and that such an outpouring will enable him to draw near the excellence of the beatitudes. She then describes both gifts and beatitudes as two sets of military skills linked (through a fanciful bit of exegesis) in a verse from Ecclesiastes, 11:2, "Divide [your grain] into seven portions or eight."[179] Seemingly, then, both gifts and beatitudes are the means of preparing one's self for the mature stage of the Christian life, with the gifts of the Holy Spirit marking the earlier stage of growth and leading to the greater excellence of the evangelical beatitudes. She makes this explicit in Book VI,[180] stating that the gifts and the beatitudes together form a program of fifteen steps. "I urge you to ascend the fifteen steps through the seven formative gifts and the eight beatitudes; ascend them in order

---

[179] "Da partem septem, necnon et octo" (IV, 4, 39–40).

[180] Book VI is primarily an exercise in numerology, perhaps designed to help William remember all that has been taught to him. Here, when she is precisely concerned about number, she makes explicit her understanding of the sequential nature of the moral program based on the gifts of the Holy Spirit and the beatitudes.

and thoughtfully, a step at a time, but vigorously, my son."[181]   What emerges from Dhuoda's development, then, is her understanding that a) the gifts and the beatitudes do belong together, but as an extended sequence rather than as parallel to one another; b) the gifts precede the beatitudes in Christian moral development because they aid in the formation of a personal and interior spirituality; and c) Christian moral development reaches perfection in the assumption of adult responsibility for the creation of the Kingdom of God within the social and political realities of one's place in the world. For her, the final stage of moral development is described by the beatitudes which are essentially the social virtues of the adult Christian.

The specific strategies which Dhuoda designs for corresponding with the gifts of the spirit reveal the very practical way in which she understood the moral life of the Christian (IV, 4). To be open to the gift of wisdom, one must love God totally, study the Scriptures avidly and put what is read into noble action. Understanding involves continued scrutiny of the Word of God with a particular emphasis upon appreciating the threat of punishment and the glory of the Kingdom. To be given counsel, seek counsel; to seek counsel effectively, keep a steady course through adversity and prosperity. The spirits of fortitude and of knowledge translate, for Dhuoda, into truisms that reflect virtually nothing of the particularities of her own experience: be strong against vice, humble in heart and chaste in body. Though Dhuoda acknowledges the importance of external action (as well as interior progress) in moral formation, her description of these early gifts follows Augustine's stress on individual perfection. But in regard to the gifts of piety and fear of the Lord, she begins to make a transition to the social order which is at once the context and the goal of personal moral growth. Piety retains something of its classical

---

[181] "In has septemplices formantium dona et in has octo partium beatitudines, per quindecies graduum militando, te, gradatim, ortor, meditanter paulatim ascenderis, fili, ut ad centesimum de laeua in dextram, ad perfectionis acumen faciliter ualeas transcurrere illaesus" (VI, 4, 43–47).

Roman sense: it is a way of fulfilling the obligations of fidelity in social relationships with a particular emphasis on generosity toward those over whom one has been given social responsibility. Dhuoda advises William, in piety, to have fraternal compassion for the neighbor, practice hospitality, console the poor and the sorrowful. Fear of the Lord, on the other hand, means appropriate respect for all those to whom the social order gives precedence: fear and love for ancestors, elders, leaders and, finally, all those equal to William in rank, whether among the older or younger members of his class. The one who is imbued with fear of the Lord will not give offense to any group, nor join in the scandalous conflicts which too often mark the relations between one social group and another. Ultimately, piety and fear of the Lord form a virtuous unit involving respect for the social order and the promotion of that peace and harmony which ought to mark the Christian *res publica.* The one who possesses these gifts is already on the way to that morality of social responsibility which will be more fully developed in Dhuoda's analysis of the life of the beatitudes.

Dhuoda ends this chapter with some general remarks on the nature of the Holy Spirit and its gifts, remarks which are primarily a catena of verses from the Scriptures. She notes that the Spirit fills the whole world, that good actions confer the Spirit on us in a permanent way and that we may keep the gifts of the Spirit with us by prayer and by keeping custody over our hearts and our speech. She speaks a great deal, here and elsewhere, about individual merits; here she says that the Holy Spirit dispenses gifts "according to the merits of each individual," but she quotes Paul to the Romans in this regard and thereby somewhat alleviates the quasi-Pelagianism of her thought. She emphasizes, as Paul did, the unity of the Spirit behind the diversity of the gifts as well as the power of the spirit manifested in what appear to be the "merits" of the individual Christian. Looked at schematically, Dhuoda's interpretation of the gifts of the Spirit proceeds from love for God and the study of the Scriptures to good actions, in general, and then to actions that are specifically described in terms of the whole of the social order (compassion and hospitality on the one hand and reverence for the social order itself on the other). Though she has kept the original order of gifts in the Isaian text, in contrast to Augustine, Dhuoda's general sense of the progress of the spiritual life, under the gifts, is not so very different from his. Augustine begins with the fear of the Lord and progresses from humility to the study of Scripture, thence to working for justice and showing of mercy in order to arrive at wisdom, which Augustine equates with peacemaking. But Dhuoda has separated the gifts from the beatitudes and in this differs most significantly from Augustine.

Dhuoda analyzes the beatitudes in Chapter 8 of Book III, which is introduced by the following heading: "That you may easily conquer vices, read with your mouth the eight beatitudes as you find them here and always keep them in your heart." To Dhuoda, reading was always reading aloud, essentially a physical activity. Thus had Augustine understood it and, in the *Confessions*, notes Ambrose's practice of silent reading as something to be wondered at. When Benedict speaks of *lectio divina* in the *Rule*, he is clearly describing reading aloud, the physical nature of which was seen as essential to the learning process. As Jean LeClercq says when he notes the importance of reading aloud in the monastic tradition, "To speak, to think, to remember, are the three necessary phases of the same activity. To express what one is thinking and to repeat it enables one to imprint it on one's mind."[182]

This kind of learning is intimately connected to action; it is acquired in a preliminary way through the action of reading and it is deepened and developed by the implementation of what is read. Dhuoda assumes that reading the beatitudes can lead William to "conquer vices more easily" because to read rightly is to practice what is read. Practical experience both completes the learning process and leads to a deeper understanding of the text. The ideal of Christian wisdom which Dhuoda has inherited from the tradition is a fusion of theory and praxis, mutually informative and

---

[182] *The Love of Learning and the Desire for God: A Study of Monastic Culture*, trans. Catharine Misrahi (New York: Fordham University Press, 1961), 21.

interdependent. Because of this, the Matthean text of the beatitudes becomes an *instrument* of moral development, not just an expression of its highest ideal. Further, at the beginning of the chapter, Dhuoda subtly indicates that her explanation will lead to a new, concrete *interpretation* of the text, appropriate for William's situation. It is not the beatitudes as he finds them in the New Testament but as he finds them *here* ("hic inveneris") that will effectively lead William to moral growth. Dhuoda is not loathe to send William to the sacred text; indeed, she exhorts him in many places to read and study the Scriptures themselves. But here it is a question of her interpretation, her practical theology, to which she bids him attend and the importance of which she underscores at the outset.

It is in this chapter that we see most clearly Dhuoda's attempts to structure a realistic spirituality for a noble layman; it is replete with references to the concrete historical realities of her world. A simple literary structure controls Dhuoda's chapter on the beatitudes.[183] There are three sets of three injunctions each, which give direct, practical explanations and applications of the thought of selected beatitudes. To make her little pattern complete, especially since she omits the beatitude on mourning, she repeats the beatitude on meekness twice and adds two psalm verses which are in the form of the beatitudes. Her freedom in arranging the text and interpreting it to suit her purposes is obvious. In each case, the third "beatitude" of the triad (sometimes, in fact, a verse chosen from the Psalms) becomes a springboard for the longer development of a theme which she considers of particular importance in William's life and in which she demonstrates her theological imagination and exegetical powers. Two themes especially capture Dhuoda's theological interest. To illustrate the importance of justice and the significance of poverty, she interrupts the simple rhythms of her prose, moving from direct exhortation to constructive, practical theology.

---

[183] See Appendix Five.

The admonitions on loving justice and acting justly within the court system, while they are heavily laced with a series of biblical sentences, nevertheless reveal the concrete juridical situation which William would encounter as a magnate. Dhuoda is both clear and exacting as she warns William against using the court system to defraud others and worsen the lot of the poor. William's aristocratic responsibilities give him the opportunity for "preparing evil traps, by composing, ordering or consenting to anything unjust [and] unmerciful merely out of the desire for perishable things."[184] To be just, however, demands of William more than an *individual* commitment to probity in court. His position and power makes him responsible for the actions of those who serve under him; unjust judgements were obviously a matter of collusion and conspiracy and William would have been in a position to be both bribed and solicited for his cooperation by the unscrupulous. Dhuoda is particularly firm in exposing his responsibility to monitor the actions of others. She reminds William that "every iniquity and injustice doubles back upon its author."[185] Justice is social; everyone who occupies a position of social importance answers for the moral behavior of his subordinates. Reward and punishment are also social; both those who do the evil and those who consent to it "are similarly tormented and tumble into the depths, if they do not correct one another."[186]

But when those in power cooperate for justice, when, indeed, they hunger for justice together, they are satisfied together. The image of reward is the banquet table, on which satisfying bread

---

[184] "Absit a te ut, pro caducis concupiscentiarum rerum, animam quam uerus et mundus et ueram et mundam atque immortalem in tuo misit fragili corpore manentem, tu, ob iniustitiis et inmisericordiis aliquid iniuste componendo, dictando etiam et consentiendo, illa laqueis praepares malis" (IV, 8, 137–42).

[185] "Omnis namque iniquitas atque iniustitia in suum pro certo recurrit auctorem" (IV, 8, 148–49).

[186] ". . . simulque in culpis, si non utrumque emendauerint, similes torquentur uoluentes ad ymma" (155–56).

abounds, a table that is also a table for one's family, surrounded with "your children like young olive plants,"[187] the sons praising and blessing the Lord. The theme of satiety and fruitfulness is echoed in an image of "the watered garden here on earth, fruitful in oil and wine."[188] So great are the rewards of justice that Dhuoda commends William to move to the perfection of justice, which is mercy. Mercy practiced on earth calls forth eternal mercy from "the most kind God." Dhuoda glosses the beatitude with a practical recommendation: William is to advance the cause of mercy in every business dealing in which he has a part.[189] She quotes an otherwise unknown hymn that links mercy and meekness and illustrates, in a telling fashion, how both are subverted by the collusion of unjust judges.[190]

For Dhuoda, all of the beatitudes, essentially social in every way, are summed up in one's attitude toward material possessions. Greed is what subverts Christian virtue and the practice of the beatitudes. Generosity guarantees moral probity, especially for one in William's social position, responsible for the affairs of a large and largely self-contained social world. Dhuoda is aware that the evangelical counsel of poverty could pose a problem for a nobleman such as William. He must not think, first of all, that only the economically poor are poor or that the dangers of material possessions are only a threat to the rich. The soul of the rich person may indeed be impoverished through vice while the poor person

---

[187] ". . . ut filii oliuarum plantationis nouellae. . ." (209–10). Here she echoes Pss 127 and 143.

[188] ". . . anima tua quasi ortus erit irriguus, oleoque et vino fecunda. . . " (197–98). Possibly a reflection of Jer 31:12.

[189] "In omni etenim negotio utilitatis, formam mitis semper incedere festina" (223–24).

[190] "Mitis corpus conteret suum,/ Manus illustris animis fultor,/ Condix glutino agitatur aulae" (225–27).

may be rich in virtue.[191] On the other hand, material possessions corrupt both rich and poor, making the poor person envious and the rich insensitive to others. Quoting a source unknown to contemporary scholars,[192] she notes that neither the rich nor the poor sleep peacefully: the one worries about how to keep what he has and the other, how to acquire what he does not.[193] In a short, acidic personal reference, she compares the envious poor to the illiterate, who wish they could read and write but do not take the necessary pains to learn.[194] We are meant to remember her own difficulties in this regard, confessed with some eloquence in an earlier chapter. It is clear that, in citing God's determination to hear the complaints of the poor, Dhuoda does not intend to romanticize the underclass. As individual moral persons, both rich and poor are susceptible to the corruption of greed. It is William's social role, as magnate and therefore the dispenser of both material goods and just judgments, which requires him to have a special regard for the poor. Dhuoda returns to this theme repeatedly in the central section of her *Liber*.

In the context of her teaching on the beatitudes, she develops a theological argument in support of the obligations of generosity incumbent on the aristocracy.[195] In this argument, she enlarges

---

[191] IV, 8, 51–56.

[192] Neither Bowers nor Riché can identify the quote, though Riché hears echoes of Gregory the Great in the *Moralia in Job* XV, 56, 65, *PL* 75, 1114c as well as echoes of Ps 49. I find the Psalm reference unconvincing.

[193] "Diues et pauper simul peribunt, simulque in egestate torquescunt, diues non largiens, pauper non habens. Cum dormierint, aequali pensu praegrauantur pondere. . . ." (58–60).

[194] "Et est pauper diuitias condens perfacile manu. Est diues inuidens pauperi, est pauper cupiens effici diues, sicut indoctus litteratus effici malens uult omnino nec ualet" (55–58).

[195] She divides it into two somewhat lengthy pieces of instruction, one after the first triad of beatitudes and the other at the conclusion of the chapter.

upon the transitory nature of material possessions (especially in comparison with eternal rewards and punishments). She affirms the reality of God's ownership of all the earth and its goods (for which the rich are God's stewards). She notes that God has inextricably linked divine generosity to the practice of liberality and is therefore the covenanted ally of the poor. Finally she develops the notion of the commonality of all people, sons and daughters of Adam and Eve who share the same fleshly condition, the same origin and the same eternal destiny. About the transitory nature of possessions, Dhuoda is specific and trenchant: "Someone may shine with gold, gems and the royal purple, but will go forth to the shadows naked and poor, carrying nothing unless he has lived well, piously, chastely, and worthily."[196] The trappings of power and position are not only transitory, however; they are visible signs of the burden of stewardship: those to whom wealth and position are given bear the responsibility for equitable distribution of the goods of creation. Dhuoda reprises here a significant tradition of the classical Christian writers of the first four centuries. Like a refrain, Dhuoda reminds William that he has received his riches from God's hand and must share what he has received "with a generous hand." "Whatever God has given, be it much or little, share it with equal grace with those who ask."[197] The first-fruits of William's substance belong to God and, beyond that, to the poor.[198] William's authority (position) comes from the same God who exhorts him to

---

[196] "Et licet homo auro, gemisque et purpura nitescat, uilis et nudus ibit ad umbras, nichil tollens secum, nisi quod bene, quod pie, quod caste, quod digne uixerit ipse" (185–88).

[197] "Sed si quid tibi Deus dederit, multum atque etiam exiguum, secundum qualitatem habendi, ita porrige petenti" (233–35).

[198] "Tu ergo, fili, honora in primis Dominum, ut aid Salomon, de tua substantia et de primitiis tuis, ceterumque rerum opum tuarum da pauperibus" (242–44). Dhuoda quotes Prov 3:9.

"give and it will be given to you."[199] The theme of stewardship, that the one who has received much must, in fairness, become a generous donor, holds together the many injunctions of this section of text.

Stewardship is even more important when considered in light of the common human condition. Dhuoda develops this theme in two directions. First, William is told to consider what he would need were he to be struck with complete indigence like the person who may ask his help. This may be a concrete warning rather than a pious admonition. Dhuoda speaks elsewhere in the book of the variations in human fortune which have brought her own family into insignificance; further, her husband Bernard continues to play a dangerous game of his own with the fortunes of history. She may well be warning William that his hold on the power to dispense favors is tenuous. But, secondly, she is also aware of the implications of the theology of creation (on which the notion of stewardship is based). She speaks explicitly of "the fraternal condition which results from our common origin."[200] Whatever their place in the social order, "all come to the same end, returning to the dust."[201] Compassion for others, then, is "fraternal compassion;" she reminds William as Moses had reminded the Israelites (and using the appropriate Old Testament quotations) that compassion for pilgrims and strangers rests on the truth that such

---

[199] "Habes auctoritatem qui tibi cum ceteris ut des admonens dicit: Date, et dabitur uobis" (252–54).

[200] "Carnem hic fraternam conditionem designat, ex qua nos cum omnibus originem trahimus, ipsi dicente protoplasto sibi simili iuncto. . ." (IV, 9, 22–24). I extend the discussion here into Chapter 9. It is a short chapter which completes Dhuoda's thought on the poor and brings all of Book IV to a close.

[201] ". . . tam pauper quam diues, omnes per finem, in puluerem reuertentur" (IV, 9, 27–28).

are "our brothers" and "our fathers."[202] The sense of family which is so pervasive through Dhuoda's entire text is extended here to the entire family of God, all those who trace their lineage back to the "first-born creature," and who now find themselves in need. William, himself, is the needy person and may one day find himself more needy still. When that day comes he will pray to God and his prayers will be validated by his compassion and generosity.

Appropriately, then, Dhuoda ends her study of the beatitudes with an explanation of the Christian practice of almsgiving. She quotes Sirach to remind William that as water extinguishes fire, so does almsgiving destroy his own sinfulness (3:33). The three-fold division of alms-giving which she describes is a kind of summary of all the duties she has just elaborated. The first duty of almsgiving is to give secretly to the poor; the secrecy will ensure that William is acting out of Christian love and preserving his own poverty of spirit. The second duty of almsgiving is to forgive in Christ those who have done you harm. Almsgiving requires, thirdly, that one correct his own faults by words and scourging even while he corrects and monitors the faults of those who are his companions and subordinates. In the practical, social morality which Dhuoda teaches her son, consistent action in the world is the substance of sanctification. But William cannot be expected to live and act in the complex, real world, without incurring some moral guilt. He will often have to choose between two evils, adjudicate in morally ambiguous cases and be responsible for the behavior of numerous soldiers whose behavior in battle and outside of it will often be corrupted by anger and greed. Hence he must look to minimize his culpability in whatever ways Scripture recommends, especially by giving his own wealth to the poor.

Dhuoda's moral world is that of the strife-ridden late Carolingians. Her program for moral development is tailored to the

---

[202] "Nam omnes nos, ut ait Scriptura, aduenae sumus, incolae et peregrini, sicut patres nostri uoluentium in terra. Lege Mosaicae admonitionis Israeli filios ad compassionem satiari fraternam. . ." (IV, 8, 33–37).

specific responsibilities of a young, aristocratic warrior. To teach him appropriately, she mines the Scriptures and the tradition with conventional pedagogy but with personal creativity. The beatitudes speak to her of the social and political realities within which she lives and they describe the mature holiness of a responsible, worldly Christian. With a confidence that comes from her intimate knowledge of her son's development and of the world they share, she does not hesitate to shape the prevailing moral tradition to his needs. Like Alcuin for Wido, she reworks the traditional catalog of virtues and vices, emphasizing those vices of most danger to her son by her practical explanation and lively, realistic examples. With a new sense of the worldly dimensions of Christian asceticism, like the bishops and abbots of her time, she significantly modifies the work of those masters, like Augustine, who were the foundations of contemporary theology. Doing theology in the classical mode, that is, with her starting point in the experience of her intended audience, she interprets Scripture and reinterprets earlier theologians carefully but firmly. She is an eloquent witness to a theological tradition that was not confined to episcopal palaces nor to the academic enclosure, but permeated the lives of lay Christians.

Chapter Five

BIBLICAL WISDOM: OBEDIENCE AND CONFLICT OF LOYALTIES[203]

Undoubtedly it was a truism of ninth century morality that the proper and primary obligation of a Christian knight was to honor and obey the natural hierarchy of the social order, and to give proper allegiance to God, the king and all others in authority in due measure. But in the dynastic wars that divided the Frankish kingdom after the death of Louis the Pious, the nobility came face to face with the moral ambiguity at the heart of that obligation. The very incident which provoked Dhuoda to write the *Liber Manualis* was a result of the changing pattern of alliances which bound her family. William had just been taken from her so that he could serve as a pledge of the good intentions of his father, Bernard, toward Charles, the youngest son of Louis the Pious. He was a kind of hostage meant to assure Charles that Bernard's allegiance, heretofore ambiguous, was now firmly fixed. For the moment, therefore, Charles was the feudal lord of both father and son. But in a time of civil war and changing boundaries, feudal allegiances were very much in flux. In such a shifting universe, could a Christian knight find moral political ground on which to stand? In Book III of the *Liber Manualis*, Dhuoda attempts to unravel the tangled skein of obligations incumbent upon William, her son, and to point him toward a course of action that is both morally defensible and politically practical. She sets out the principles and

---

[203] An earlier and briefer version of this chapter was presented at the National Meeting of the College Theology Society, May, 1992.

strategies by which William can discover that ground and occupy it.

Dhuoda begins by defining and describing the hierarchy of obligations within which William lives. In this hierarchy, the mandates of the divine will are foundational and without qualification: nothing may be done against one's obligation to God, the ultimate feudal lord. Among human authorities, Dhuoda affirms the absolute primacy of the father; only obligations to God may take precedence over obligations to one's father, and all other obligations are contingent upon these. Therefore, in Book III of the *Liber Manualis*, Dhuoda first lays out William's absolute duties to his father (under God) and his contingent obligations to Charles, his father's overlord and his own. At the end of Book III, she completes her description of the feudal hierarchy by describing in short, specific chapters, William's responsibilities to the King's relatives, the nobility of various ranks and the priests.

Recourse to a theoretical hierarchy of obligations alone will not, however, ensure William's safe and righteous conduct. Threading his way through this tangle requires a canny, not to say cunning, practicality. In Dhuoda's mind, it also requires virtue and spiritual discipline as well, because success at court is a moral task as well as a practical one and involves more than merely having an eye to the main chance. Dhuoda's plan for resolving the moral ambiguity within the complex of feudal obligations thus becomes a strategic plan that involves both action and asceticism. According to Dhuoda, that which cannot be easily solved at the level of theory may be worked through on the level of practical action. But in order to act morally under the various pressures attendant upon him, William must be deeply rooted in a disciplined and thoughtful Christian life. The key to Dhuoda's moral program is William's participation in the office of the royal counsellor. Therefore the central section of Book III, its core as it were, is devoted to developing in significant detail the position of counsellor and the ways in which it determines the ascetical and moral development of a Christian knight.

Book III, then, composed of eleven chapters, can be approached through its four major themes: William's obligations to his father, his obligations to his feudal lord, the role of counsellor and William's obligations to others in the higher levels of the feudal hierarchy. The development here is modestly logical, in spite of Dhuoda's disclaimer about her ability to compose a systematic work.[204] Dhuoda has organized Book III so that her central concern, in this case the role of royal counsellor, is in the center of the book, with chapters on the variety of feudal obligations before and after. A more logical order of investigation, however, is to analyze Dhuoda's understanding of the full range of feudal obligations before focussing attention, where she does, on the vocation of the counsellor and its appropriate spirituality.

A discernible literary pattern controls each of the small chapters that comprise Book III. Each chapter begins with a direct and forceful admonition about a particular responsibility incumbent upon William. This is followed immediately by biblical and/or practical rationale, generally short and pertinent. The bulk of each chapter consists in a more detailed exposition of the admonition. This often involves some discussion of biblical or historical models of behavior, the giving of more specific and/or more practical content to the admonition, a discussion of the moral tensions involved, and exploration of the theological implications and a more careful development of the motivations which Dhuoda hopes to awaken in William. Finally, each chapter concludes with a prayer, based very specifically on the content of the admonition. This prayer is often a clear hermeneutical key to her moral emphasis in the chapter. Within this simple, flexible format, Dhuoda develops her thought on the obligations of fidelity, the moral dimension of the role of counsellors and William's specific obligations to the various categories of persons within his feudal world.

---

[204] I, 4, 14–16.

William's Obligations to His Father

William's obligations to his father open Book III and subsequently shape its content; they are very simply stated in the first line of Chapter One. William must *fear, love* and *be faithful* to his father in all things.[205] As she develops her thought, this simple, almost trite, moral principle is nuanced by her allusions to the specific circumstances in which William finds himself. Though Dhuoda places Bernard first, after God, in the order of obligations, her admonition is not to a slavish or thoughtless obedience. Quoting Sirach 3 and 7, she speaks first of the respect which comes to a father from a morally upright son: William is to receive his father in old age and not sadden him by a dissolute life. She thus indicates that the duty of obedience is paid, most importantly, in the currency of character. She also underlines Sirach's advice that a son not show contempt for a father who may grow weaker precisely as the former reaches the apex of his strength (III, 1, 17–19). With this simple biblical reference, Dhuoda points to the changing situation between father and son: William is now at court, in the very center of power, while Bernard is still in the military field, subject to the vicissitudes of battle. William must not become arrogant, but reflect even more deeply on the obligations he owes his father. These are the internal dispositions which William must cultivate; in practical affairs, Dhuoda recommends that William heed Bernard's judgment (16–17). What he owes Bernard is respect that is "proper, faithful and sure."[206] Not only is there room here for discernment; his very filial obligations demand such discernment. In Dhuoda's mind, the primary obedience which William owes to his father is to grow in true wisdom and to acquire a mature, firm and thoughtful moral character. At the very beginning of her discussion, she thus lays the groundwork for what

---

[205] Qualiter domno et genitori tuo Bernardo, tam praesens quam absens, timere, amare, atque fidelis in omnibus esse debeas. . ." (III, 1, 3–5).

[206] "proprium, fidelem et certum" (III, 2, 10-11).

follows and sounds an important note. The whole of Book III is Dhuoda's coherent argument that William must become a mature Christian with acute moral sensibilities. This is not just a strategy for finding his way out of a moral thicket; it is the logical consequence of his primary moral obligation to his father.

In Dhuoda's mind, William owes Bernard obedience not only because he is the source of William's life, but also because he is the source of his *rank*. Dhuoda sets this thought apart in a short chapter (Chapter 2) as if she would give it a particular importance. Small though it is, the chapter is full of tensions and ambiguities. She asserts that rank is fixed and is of divine origin; this assertion is both descriptive and, perhaps, a veiled warning. Though, in the world, people are venerated because of the offices and titles conferred by human authority, William is to honor the rank which comes to him by birth, a kind of double gift of both his father and God, the giver of life.[207] Dhuoda notes her own divergence from the received wisdom here and suggests the cause the dynastic wars of her day: the sons of Louis the Pious, not content with the titles and offices they had been *given* nor with the rank to which they had been born, have cast their world into the chaos of civil war. It is *against* this human ambition that William is to act; let him remember that he must first love God and, after that, his father. Her assumption seems to be that the remembrance of God's prior claim on his allegiance and of the divine source of his rank by birth will be the means by which William will understand his place in the feudal universe and be content with it. This will not entirely solve the problem of conflicting loyalties, but Dhuoda identifies an

---

[207] In a footnote to her translation, Neel says that "Dhuoda's remarks here about the insignificance of worldly power show some confusion. She generally argues that temporal and spiritual preferment are parallel" (122, n.25). Indeed, but her task in this entire book is to give William the ability to negotiate *conflicting* claims on his obedience. In that critical moment, spiritual values, here defined as the God-given authority of his father, must prevail. This is reinforced by some of the biblical models she chooses in this section of her text.

unholy ambition as the source of the conflicts and she counsels William to cut off the disease at its source.

In attempting to motivate William to appropriate obedience, Dhuoda gives full play to her powers of persuasion. Her counsel is sharpened by her awareness of the temptations with which William is surrounded. In Book III, 1, she urgently warns William to avoid two specific kinds of disobedience, both of which she has "heard" and/or "read" about. These sins are 1) to cause grief to one's father in his old age (Eccl 3:15) and 2) to inflict harm on one's father, insulting his dignity (Deut 27:16). In both cases, she disclaims any possibility that William could even consider such evil, but she warns of the evil companions which may attend him at court, companions who are themselves caught up in the general spirit of civil factions and treachery. In such an atmosphere, William will have to exercise great care in dealing with "such people, if there are any, which may God forbid."[208] She piles up biblical reasons for filial obedience as well as reasons based on the structure of society. She makes her own the scriptural curse against the disobedient son (III, 1, 34–37), though she does remind William that even the most flagrantly unfaithful may be brought to repentance and, hence, to salvation (50–52). Her text here is intense; it is difficult not to read between the lines the fear of a mother who knows both the possibility and the dire consequences of betrayal.

To reinforce her own arguments Dhuoda mines the wisdom of a variety of Old Testament books. The predominance of Old Testament references throughout Book III is significant. In a line of thinkers from Augustine to Calvin and along with her contemporaries, Dhuoda has recourse to the narratives of the kingdom of Israel when, as a colleague of mine put it, Jesus fails her as a state advisor. Indeed, the silence of Jesus on matters political does not seem at all strange to her. From Sirach, she takes the reminder that without his father, William would not have life

---

[208] "Et si sunt tales, quod absit. . . " (III, 1, 50).

(7:28). From Exodus, the promise that those who honor their fathers are granted long lives (Exod 20:12). The Pentateuch supplies curses for those who are unfaithful (Deut 27:16 and Lev 20:9) and reinforces the negative message gleaned from the examples of Absalom and the sons of Heli.[209] She sums up biblical evidence to conclude that all manner of evil befalls the disobedient child: envy, jealousy and disaster are their portion and, the ultimate irony, they lose all the material possessions which they sought, by infidelity, to gain.[210] These biblical allusions are scattered like the lines of a refrain throughout the first two chapters of Book III. Then, like a coda, she ends the section on filial obedience with a kind of catalog of the wisdom of the patriarchs (III, 3). She culls from Genesis the stories of the faithful sons (Sem, Isaac, Jacob and Joseph) and piles up the list of blessings which they achieved through their obedience: prosperity; deliverance from sorrow; happiness; fortitude and the overcoming of temptation; a wife, children and riches; safety amidst the vicissitudes of life. In the composition of this catalog, Dhuoda is careful to show how both worldly and spiritual blessings are given to loyal children. At the same time, in the story of the patriarch Joseph, she shows that the path of the obedient will not be without pitfalls. Joseph's way led, after all, through a very deep pit. But at the end, for him, there was the opportunity to rule in a *peaceful* kingdom. This, for Dhuoda, is the ultimate blessing, both spiritual and secular. Wallace-Hadrill notes that "when a Carolingian wanted a picture of how a God-directed king should behave, his attention was directed to the Old Testament. . . ."[211] It is clear from the entire *Liber Manualis*, but particularly this Book, that Dhuoda also saw the Old Testament texts as containing the necessary practical wisdom for her own day

---

[209] As Riché notes, Rhabanus Maurus had used the same biblical models to reinforce the same political and familial themes. See *Liber de reuerentia filiorum erga patres et erga reges*. MGH Epist 5, 403–5.

[210] III, 1, 20–47.

[211] *Early Medieval History* (New York: Harper and Row, 1976), 184.

and aristocratic circle. It was not just the king who found his true ancestors in the historical books of the Jews. Other powerful Christians were also the spiritual descendants of the biblical characters of old. The Kingdom of God, for Dhuoda, began in Israel, was given a particular character in the New Testament, and continued in the Frankish Kingdom of her day. So thoroughly does she rely on Old Testament texts in her book that we cannot escape the impression that she interpreted her own times as particularly congruent with Old Testament times. Nowhere is this more true than when she seeks to understand and to ameliorate the civil factions and treachery of the circles of the court.

William's Obligations to Charles

In contrast to her explanation of William's obligations to his father, her chapter on his fidelity to his feudal lord (Chapter 4) is brief, less intense and better organized. Here the general format described above is faithfully adhered to; in it, Dhuoda demonstrates that she is as circumspect as she bids William to be. She begins with the simple admonition that William serve his lord in all practical matters with *prudence*, seeking not to "please the eye" but to preserve both true loyalty and purity of body and soul. This is a most difficult balance to which she exhorts William throughout the chapter. On the one hand, William's service to Charles must be fixed, loyal and without reservation;[212] toward his lord he must always be true, alert, helpful and the first to step forward in service.[213] On the other hand, William must be truly prudent, considering not only what will serve Charles' immediate purposes, but what will also preserve his own conscience and honor God, who is the Lord of all.

---

[212] "puram et certam illi in omnibus tene utilitatis fidem" (III, 4, 8–9).

[213] "seniori ut praedixi tuo sis uerax, uigil, utilisque atque praecipuus" (4, 38–39).

The rationale with which Dhuoda supports her admonition is primarily practical and on the side of true and faithful service. William is to serve Charles because he has been chosen as Lord by both Bernard and God (4, 2–3). Here again we see Dhuoda's conviction that the hierarchy of the Frankish world reflects the divine will. Such fidelity to feudal obligations is also the family tradition and honor. She points out to William that such an obligation of nobility comes to him from both sides of his ancestry (5–6); for Dhuoda, nobility does indeed oblige. She warns William that public opinion always treats the unfaithful servant unmercifully, but insists that she is not concerned about William or the soldiers who are in his personal service. No one in his family was ever unfaithful, nor are they now, nor will they ever be (32–36). Though the words express confidence, their impassioned repetition reminds the reader of Bernard's recent equivocation and turns this affirmation into a warning, for Bernard as well as for William. Dhuoda points out that society considers treachery reprehensible; she also hopes and prays that William's aristocratic family traditions will make it unthinkable. To the familial tradition, Dhuoda adds her reading of the theological tradition. Using Romans 13: 1–2, a verse much commented on in the eighth and ninth centuries, Dhuoda points out that all office and power are given by God and therefore William's service must be faithful, wholehearted and energetic (22–25). The *explicit* teaching is clear and unqualified, but the array of biblical models which she gathers maintain the moral tension inherent in her original admonition. She cites the servant of Abraham sent to get a wife for Isaac, Joab, Abner and the other servants of David as well as "many others in Scripture." On the one hand, the obedience of these models brought them material blessings and a good name "in the world." On the other hand, they themselves underwent trials and tribulations in their attempt to please their lords rather than themselves (14–19). William must be prepared for the difficulties and moral ambiguities of feudal service as well as for its blessings.

In Chapter 4, Dhuoda demonstrates that faithful service is not an obvious or slavish following of royal commands. It is a *virtue* that must be learned and acquired. Therefore, she bids William to read both the lives and the sayings of the Fathers. Her emphasis on the *lives* of holy ancestors is important. It is not just words of wisdom which William needs but the concrete example of those who have demonstrated practical prudence. William must study the ways in which successful predecessors negotiated the moral ambiguities of their own time so that he can, as she puts it, "learn in what manner and in what measure one ought to serve."[214] Measure is equally important with manner; neither can be learned entirely in the abstract, and so the *lives* of holy predecessors are important evidence. The study of such evidence, according to Dhuoda, leads to a true and practical understanding; only when understanding has been gained, must William be *zealous* in fulfilling his duty (44–45). Finally, Dhuoda recommends that William study his contemporaries as well. Though she often decries the moral degeneration of her time, she is still convinced that there are many good and upright Christians at court whose example can help to form her son. She bids William seek those who are consistently faithful so that he might learn from them true service (45–47). But Dhuoda ends this chapter on service to his lord, as always, by reminding William that his best teacher in the ways of true and prudent service is God. She prays that both God and his lord may be to William as a tutor, monitor, protector, helper and defender. He will need all of this support as he wends his way through the moral thicket of the court. Her last words are "Sicut fuerit uoluntas in coelo, sic fiat. Amen." It is a direct quotation from 1 Macc 3:60 which, as Riché points out, forms the responsorial for the Monday office. But it also echoes the well-known line from Matthew's form of the dominical prayer. In both contexts, the words are a prayer that the will of God which governs heaven may also govern earthly activities. Thus her advice on

---

[214] "Lege dictas uel uitas sanctorum praecedentium patrum, et inuenies qualiter uel quomodo tuo seniori debeas seruire atque fidelis adesse in omnibus" (41–44).

service to lord ends with a powerful reminder of the moral sovereignty of God.

Others in the Feudal Hierarchy

Though feudal ethics and custom bound William primarily to both his father and his lord, the social and spiritual world as Dhuoda knew it comprised a wider range of relationships; to these Dhuoda turns her attention in the last four chapters of Book III. Chapters 8 and 9 speak of William's obligations to the relatives of his lord and to the highest leaders of the realm. Nothing in these two chapters really adds to what Dhuoda has taught in Chapter 4. What William owes to his lord, he owes, with slight modification, to his lord's family, that is, respect and faithful submission. Charles' family shares in his vocation; they too have been chosen by God to share the responsibility for the kingdom (III, 8, 40–42).[215] Therefore William may use toward all of them the same biblical models of conduct—namely, Abraham, Isaac, Jacob, and David. There is, in fact, a rather poignant reference to the fidelity of David, who honored Jonathan, the son of King Saul, even in death. Though she utters a fervent plea that William's fidelity will not bring him to such sadness, she paints the fidelity of David in such touching detail, with mention of his tenderness and tears, that it seems to suggest a real possibility to her (11–24). To the other magnates and counsellors, whoever is of equal rank to William and "of importance at court," he owes "love, affection and service." From them, at least from some of them, William can learn the virtues proper to the nobility: humility, charity, chastity, patience, gentleness, moderation, sobriety and astuteness (III, 9, 9–11). The list bears a strong resemblance to Paul's list of the fruits of the

---

[215] Though she clearly refers elsewhere in Book III to the current fighting between the various sons of Louis the Pious, Dhuoda seems to ignore here the obvious problem: that Charles' enemies are also the members of his own family. Therefore, William cannot offer to all of Charles' relatives the submission which she recommends without violating the conditions of his feudal loyalty.

Spirit (Gal 5:22–23). Her ideal of balance between personal integrity and true submission remains the leitmotif: William is so to conduct himself that he acts without even a shadow of infidelity, while, at the same time, he leads a praiseworthy life, zealous for all good works (III, 9, 15–19). Only in the prayer which concludes Chapter 8 does she reveal, by its content, some sense of the additional troubles which may arise in the world of royal relatives and noble advisors. She prays, "may those prosper who in this present time pursue peace in the manner of their fathers" (III, 8, 46–48). Perhaps she intends to discriminate here among the sons of Louis the Pious on the basis of their sincere desire for peace; she may then be encouraging and warning William to support his sovereign along this path and to side with those who opt for peace. She continues, "may there be protection against the enemies rising up on all sides" (49–51). The Christian knight must be wary not only of the obvious enemy, but of the traitor who is at one's side, or, possibly, on all sides. It is precisely against the sin of treachery that the whole of Book III is, in one way or another, addressed. Finally she prays, "May holy church be more firmly united in the faith of Christ" (51–53). Ecclesiastics who used biblical models of kingship in support of one or another of the contending factions contributed greatly to the divisions between camps and, further, divided the church itself, even in the heart of its theological self-understanding. Here Dhuoda prays for the true unity of the church; in the last chapter of Book III, she will take up the question of the church's clergy, their true role and the loyalty which they may rightfully claim from the nobility.

But before proceeding to that topic, with which she ends Book III, Dhuoda inserts a chapter on William's obligation to those of lesser rank. I say "inserts" because this chapter is a kind of foil to the others in Book III. Whereas the other chapters explicate and support the beliefs upon which the Frankish social structure was founded, that it was to those of one's own rank and of superior status that one owed fidelity and allegiance, this chapter goes beyond the accepted norms of behavior and encourages *cooperation with*, as well as condescension to, those in inferior ranks. It is a relatively lengthy and detailed chapter, full of biblical quotes and theological reasoning; Dhuoda seems to put herself out to convince William of what must have been a religious truth more honored in speech than in action. She begins by saying that she need not advise him to follow the example of those in superior ranks; this is the received wisdom. But then she gives what is the principal admonition of this chapter, that William should not fail to follow the good example of those inferior to him in rank. Further, he should join with them ("illosque tibi coniungi") in whatever is of practical benefit (III, 10, 5–8). Here, finally, we begin to find significant attention to New Testament Scripture. Indeed, this chapter as a whole is much more Christological than any others in her book and her Christological thought follows the line of Irenaeus' recapitulation soteriology. She first recalls the example of God who created all persons and then shows Christ as the fulfillment of the divine initiative, taking on the form of a servant that he might bring down the mighty and exalt the lowly (11–14). She repeats what she has insisted upon before, that all rank and authority is God-given, but she adds an important *caveat* here: everything created—rank included—is meant for the praise and glory of God, who gives special attention and blessings to the lowly (26–31). A theology of creation and a sense of nature as a unified whole pervades this chapter and gives some unity to its disparate, sometimes rambling thought. An extended allegory on the harts (80–116), an exegetical commonplace since Augustine, becomes her paradigm of the mutual support and affection to be found in nature. Each animal takes a turn supporting the others with his horns as the whole group attempts to swim a deep river. There is no consideration of status among them; each does what is necessary when the time comes. The meaning is clear to the learned, Dhuoda insists: just so ought the human community to live, each helping the other and supporting all, without distinction of rank.[216]

---

[216] "Nam in subportationem, uel uicissitudinis mutationem, dilectionem tam in maioribus quam in minoribus per compassionis fraternitatem omnimodis per

Therefore, the world of nature can be a source of *moral* teaching, because the one God is both Creator and Redeemer (117–26). She has insisted throughout Book III that the will of God forms the master plan for human society. Here she situates human society within the created cosmos, indicating that she believes human society must struggle to achieve that unity natural to the rest of the cosmos. The first step toward that goal is the service and praise which creatures endowed with reason owe to their Creator and Lord.

William is to praise God by imitating God's own example, helping those of lesser worldly importance and, as the Apostle Paul says, carrying the burdens of the weak even as he allows his own burdens to be carried by those beneath him (33–37). In the chapters on the royal counsellor, Dhuoda emphasizes a ministry of *good words*; here she stresses that good and generous deeds must reinforce and exemplify helpful words (56–57). She further superimposes an evangelical vision of mutuality and communal life upon the hierarchical structure of William's social world. She is not alone among Carolingian writers, of course, in insisting upon the permanent relevance of early apostolic ideals. But this represents a shift in the direction of Book III of the *Liber*, and this newness is reinforced by the plethora of New Testament allusions and citations which replace in this chapter her reliance upon Old Testament models in the others. At the same time, her practicality remains. She exhorts William to a practical generosity that goes beyond material goods and expresses itself in a gracious and gentle manner.[217] Her concluding prayer reiterates her primary emphasis: let the little ones come unto me, for such is the kingdom of heaven. In the midst of the various obligations to which the feudal hierarchy

---

cuncta in generi humano ostendit esse tenendam" (III, 10, 95–99).

[217] ". . . ut manus tua in operibus dignis prompta, et magnis et minimis aequalibusque atque exiguis personis prout uales habens et habere poteris unquam seruitium et honorem non solum uerbis sed et factis studeas implere, et hoc cum mansuetidinis allocutione" (53–58).

binds her son, William is not to forget the evangelical commands. Though, for Dhuoda, God's will is expressed in that hierarchy, God's *entire* will is not found there, but also in the natural world and in the Scriptures which bind William to a special concern for those of lesser rank and of limited power.

Dhuoda concludes her study of William's obligations with a chapter on priests. Though members of the higher clergy had significant political power in the Frankish kingdom and were among the counsellors of the realm, Dhuoda's reflections center primarily on their sacramental character. For her, priests are to be respected because they consecrate the chrism and oil, baptize in the name of the Trinity, consecrate bread and wine in the likeness of the body and blood of Christ, prepare the table and give communion for the remission of sins and the health of the body (III, 11, 6–12). Hers is a succinct and comprehensive summary of the sacramental system as she experienced it.[218] Her theology of priesthood is structured by the etymologies of the various titles given to priests; they are *sacerdotes, pastores, presbyteri, episcopi, speculatores,* and *pontifices.*[219] She emphasizes priestly functions: priests sanctify, feed the flock both by word and example, draw near to the altar so as to lead others there, urge all to strive for the things above and build bridges by which believers cross over the muddy waters of sin to the true homeland. She sums up this

---

[218] Note that repentance and forgiveness of sin are still associated, in her mind at least, with communion as well as with sacramental confession, although later in the chapter she recommends that William make a personal confession to the best of his ability, in order to keep the sincere soul from hell (148–50 of Chapter 11). She explicitly describes personal confession as made privately, accompanied with sighing and tears.

[219] Though she takes these etymologies from such respected sources as Rabanus Maurus, Ps-Cyprien and Isidore of Seville, she does not rigidly distinguish, as does Rabanus Maurus, for instance, between the various orders of the priesthood, between the priest as *sacerdos* or as *episcopus.* She says quite explicitly that although their titles and ranks may vary, all are properly priests and bear similar dignity.

analysis by saying that priests are the representatives of God and bear God's authority above and beneath us, within and without. From above, they watch; from below, they are the feet which bring salvation. From within, they instruct and from without, their prayers surround us like a defensive fort. Her text here echoes explicitly her description of the divine reality itself in Book I (6, 19–20), suggesting that Dhuoda believes that the priests, in all their human frailty, represent God, in all the divine grandeur.

At the same time, in discussing how William may both serve the Lord's anointed and benefit from their special character, Dhuoda does distinguish between worthy and less worthy priests. Though she strongly cautions him not to condemn those who may appear less virtuous than they should be, William is to imitate only those whom he finds to be superior in virtue and "more clearheaded in word and deed."[220] Likewise he is to entrust himself into the hands of priests who are honorable and loyal to him; these can act as his counsellors.[221] Dhuoda gives a brief picture of the social setting in which the collaboration between clergy and aristocracy could take place. She bids William dine often with good priests and with hungry pilgrims and adds that priests can be the instruments by which food and drink are offered to the poor from William's own table. In the preceding discussion of their functions, she does not mention that the priests were often almoners on behalf of the magnates, but her exhortations here show them in that function. They were a potential goad to conscience as they shared the banquets of the wealthy, bringing pilgrims with them to the table and taking food away to satisfy the hungry.

---

[220] This translation is Neel's. The Latin reads, "sensu capaciores in uerbis et factis" (III, 11, 108).

[221] "In manus. . . honestorum sacerdotum, te non pigeas commendare. Habe ex ipsis, infra ceteros fideles, congrue per tempus, consiliatores" (116–19).

The Office of Royal Counsellor

The complex network of feudal relationships which Dhuoda describes can indeed create for a young and inexperienced knight a variety of practical and moral tensions, especially since William is required to be faithful, above all, to the Lord of Heaven and Earth in all of his practical activities. As mother and teacher, Dhuoda earnestly seeks a practical program which she can teach William and which may, at least in part, help him resolve certain moral dilemmas. She finds the key to her program in the role of the royal counsellor, an institution of great importance among the Frankish nobility.[222] In the best of all possible worlds, a noble person's obligations will be made coherent by the over-arching lordship of God, whose commands to all are consistent and revealed. But in the real world, the courtly world to which William has just been sent, conflicting feudal obligations often pulled a noble warrior in more than one direction. In such a situation, he must learn to listen to good counsel and to give it. In the political institution of the counsellor, Dhuoda sees great possibilities for moral development and moral leadership, an opportunity for bringing the mandates of the divine will to bear on the practical politics of the day. She devotes three chapters to the topic of giving and receiving counsel (as she did to the topic of filial obligations) and like the former, those on the role of counsellor are dense and marked by sudden shifts of thought; she develops her thought in a circular rather than a linear fashion, returning to those ideas which most exercise her. In the first chapter, Dhuoda lays out her full argument about the role of counsellor, defining it and giving biblical and practical rationale to support her ideas. Then she adds, in a separate chapter, some very personal reflections on the possibilities of finding good

---

[222] Riché speaks, in his introduction, of the importance of this office in the ninth century. He points to the historical narratives which describe the work of the counsellors: Thegan, *Vita Ludowici*, the *Annales de S. Bertin*, and Nithard and Hincmar's advice in *De ordine palatii*, 25.

counsel. Finally, a third chapter, Chapter 7 of Book III, explores the social and communal implications of the role of counsellor. The good counsellor will succeed if he associates himself with virtuous companions; if he fails, many others will suffer with him.[223]

Chapter 5, on the Role of the Counsellor, is a kind of expanded discussion of the virtue of prudence, central to Dhuoda's understanding of feudal obedience. Here she discusses the political *office* in which the virtue of prudence may be both acquired and exercised. The opening sentence of Chapter 5 exposes the main outlines of her thought. "If at some time God leads you to such perfection that you are considered worthy to be called as a counsellor among the magnates, consider prudently what, when, to whom and how you should speak so that what you say is worthy and to the point."[224] Note that only God can give the perfection required of a counsellor; therefore the counsel to be given is of a higher order than worldly wisdom. For Dhuoda, the role of counsellor is more than a political appointment; it is a vocation, not lightly to be taken on oneself. Her thought is consistent with that of the better known Hincmar of Rheims, who distinguishes explicitly between the worldly wisdom which is inimical to God and the "just and correct wisdom" which can guide the ruler

---

[223] Wallace-Hadrill, in discussing the moral teaching given to the Frankish kings, asks: "What was the difference, then, between the virtues of the just man and those of the just king? It was difference of scale, mostly; any man might imperil the salvation of Christian society by injustice, but the king was likeliest to do so because he had entrusted to him a greater share of divine authority than had anyone else, and had the added responsibility of supervising authority delegated to those beneath him," *Early Medieval History*, 192. Dhuoda imputes the same expanded responsibility to the royal counsellor, on whose advice the king might act.

[224] "Si ad perfectum te aliquando adduxerit Deus, ut ad consilium inter magnatos merearis esse uocatus, tracta prudenter quid, quando, cui, uel quomodo dignum et aptum possis exibere sermonem" (III, 5, 2–5).

through the murky waters of human influences and temptations.[225] What Dhuoda says about counsellors is best seen as a conscious parallel to the way in which kingship theory was developed, especially under Louis the Pious. Wallace-Hadrill, in *The Frankish Church*, notes the work of what he calls "a select company of theorists" who developed a kind of professional ethics for the king conditioned by his theocratic character. All of these theoreticians, beginning with Smaragdus in his *Via Regia* and including Abbot Agobard and Bishop Jonas of Orleans, culled the biblical texts, especially the Old Testament, for examples of how to preserve the Christian character of society and ensure that God's justice was done. As Wallace-Hadrill says, "the answer of the moralists was clear: look back to the biblical rulers and see how they managed under God's guidance."[226] Dhuoda follows the same principle and the same methods of interpreting salvation history in designing her understanding of the vocation of the counsellor. Her text is evidence that these political themes and biblical methods were not restricted to professional court theologians and demonstrates her place in the central theological endeavors of her time.

In her eminently practical way, however, she emphasizes not the theoretical situation of the counsellor but the manner of giving counsel. Virtuous advice may be given, but it is not authentic counsel unless it is *effective*, that is to say, unless it is accepted. The counsel expected from the true counsellor, therefore, is that which is to the point, worthy (of divine approbation) and given with due regard to all the circumstances. She develops this idea by introducing a controlling metaphor from the world of the artisan, the successful goldsmith, who considers the time of day, the temperature and the humidity to ensure the quality, permanence

---

[225] Hinkmar von Reims, *De Ordine palatii*, (ed) Thomas Grass und Rudolf Schieffer (Hannover, 1980), Ch. 31, 507–33.

[226] *The Frankish Church* (Oxford: Clarendon Press, 1983), 239–41.

and beauty of the artifact being constructed.[227] The metaphor serves to introduce a chain of biblical references linked by their reference to "gold." Intelligent advice, she says, is purer than gold or silver (III, 5, 20, citing Prov 22:1);[228] the one who is zealous for divine practical wisdom can please both God and his lord, but will be tested like gold in the fire (30, citing Ps 11:7). Additional citations further define proper counsel and reiterate the moral and spiritual horizon against which practical actions are to be taken. She thus distinguishes "good counsel" from simple pragmatism and speaks against the principle that the end justifies the means. The means themselves are to be tested by the virtuous counsellor, and accepted only if they are consistent with the values of Scripture.

Dhuoda's understanding of the role of counsellor presupposes that the counsellor is a person of spiritual depth. An essential component of William's *moral strategy* must, therefore, be the cultivation of a spiritual life, one specifically tailored to his secular obligations.[229] She counsels William, first of all, to "cling" to God through faith, fear and love. Though the young, in the fullness of their strength, may be slow to depend entirely on God, William must not fail to do so (36–37). Only the one who remains *in Christ* ("manentem in Christo"—the phrase is thoroughly Pauline) can give advice which is both useful to human leaders and morally righteous (32–35). The counsellor rooted in Christ and intimate with God must pray incessantly for wisdom. Here Dhuoda piles up

---

[227] (5, 13–17) This is one of the few, but illuminating, windows which she opens onto her everyday life. Since Uzès was the site of a Carolingian mint, Dhuoda may well have observed the artisans there.

[228] In these chapters on the role of counsellor, her citations are most frequently from the Wisdom literature of the Old Testament. At the very heart of that literature is the understanding that "the good life" is, indeed, one carefully crafted by a spiritual artisan, adept in the Torah as in the knowledge of the human heart.

[229] This is also the point of her work on the beatitudes in Book IV of the *Liber*. There she attempts to construct a comprehensive program in the development of a worldly spirituality for William. See Chapter Five above.

a chain of biblical citations to demonstrate that such prayer is both necessary and inevitably successful. Finally, Dhuoda counsels William to seek counsel himself, not only from the elders among the advisors but also from those younger nobles who are learning to love God and act wisely (58–64). As does the *Rule of Benedict*, she cites the examples of Samuel and Daniel who were wise in their youth and, outstripping older men, gave efficacious counsel to kings, even among the pagans (66–71).

The role of counsellor as Dhuoda conceives it is not that of the isolated wise man. Throughout the *Liber Manualis* she reiterates the importance of good companions in the Christian life. Here, she insists that to be a good counsellor, William must seek the companionship of those who are wise according to the Scriptures: holy, prayerful, seeking intimacy with God. The goal of true counsel is nothing less than to achieve the Kingdom of God; the road to that Kingdom must be traveled in the company of colleagues who share one's faith and one's struggles for virtue.[230] As Dhuoda understands it, the virtuous counsellors of her own day are only the latest in a long and noble line. Therefore, she again reaches back, for specific models, to William's spiritual ancestors, the "first fathers" described in the Old Testament. She details Joseph's counsel to Pharaoh; Daniel's to Nebuchadnezzar; Belshazzar and others; Jethro's to Moses; Achior's to Holofernes (72-80). As she interprets their stories, these were counsellors who achieved the marvelous moral and practical balance which she hopes that William can also attain. They did not abandon their own kin (is there a subtle plea here that William remember his family's fortunes?), they won freedom and prosperity for themselves and others on all sides and, especially, they preserved the integrity of their consciences. She does not hesitate to reiterate to William that these counsellors did not reach such great heights without having

---

[230] Here, Dhuoda echoes Isidore of Seville, a writer she recommends to William elsewhere. In *Synonyms* II, 44, Migne, *PL* 83. 855 C,D, Isidore recommends that those who would give good counsel must seek virtuous companions, "similes enim similibus conjungi solent."

to undergo the test of suffering (a reprise of her gold-in-the-fire theme). Indeed, the Lord of the Kingdom welcomes them precisely as "sacrificial offerings."[231] Her concluding prayer, as always, is a wish that what she has just described as ideal will become the reality of William's life.

Two more chapters (6 and 7) are devoted to the role of noble counsellors. Both are relatively short and function somewhat as refrains, echoing and reinforcing two points most dear to her heart. In the first of these, a very personal chapter, Dhuoda defends herself as a good counsellor. She criticizes those who take upon themselves the role of counsellor and yet do not strive for the perfection which the role requires and which she has just described. Using Paul's words of praise for himself in 2 Cor: 11:23, she says that she is much more the true counsellor than any one of them, though, like Paul, she has not wasted her words describing her own search for perfection (III, 6, 3). Rather, her counsel speaks for itself. Unlike the counsel of others, hers gets right to heart of the matter; it takes account of all the concrete circumstances; it is therefore well-given (6-9). We are reminded of Dhuoda's example of the goldsmith and may conclude that she sees herself as a true artisan in the giving of advice.

But Dhuoda moves quickly back to the practical order for her penultimate word on royal counsellors (III, 7). Reminding William that all depends on the omnipotence of God, she repeats her earlier emphasis on the importance of good companions in the acquisition of the virtues of prudence and counsel. She exhorts William both to avoid evil companions and seek only to associate with the pious (5-6), those who give *true* submission to their Lords (42). She specifically warns him to avoid those who are, by disposition, angry and envious (III, 7, 6-7). She anticipates here her lengthy development of the virtues and vices in Book IV, where both anger

---

[231] "... ut aurum probatos sibi dinoscitur applicuisse, et uelut holocausti hostiam . . . " (III, 5, 84–86). The reference is from Wisd 3:6: "Tanquam aurum in fornace probauit illos, et quasi holocausti hostiam accepit illos."

and envy are singled out as particularly destructive to those in William's situation. Here she notes that anger and envy take away peace and security (with a rare metaphor she notes that these evils "gnaw at you like a worm") and lead inevitably to the fateful fall into the depths (7–10). It is unclear whether she speaks of the historical fall from royal favor or the eternal fall from grace. The words she uses are traditionally eschatological, but given her understanding of the intimate connection between the historical and the eternal and her earlier remarks about the fall of her family from the ranks of the historically important, she must hope that William can avoid both disasters by rejecting angry and envious companions.

Before concluding her thoughts on the role of royal counsellors, Dhuoda constructs yet another catalog of biblical models. She comments on the bad example given by Achitophel, who encouraged Absalom to rise against his father, David, and by Haman, who advised Ahasuerus to destroy the sons of Israel (11–14). In contrast, she praises Doeg the Edomite (from the First book of Samuel) and Mordecai in the Story of Esther (15–16). Evil counsellors fell victim to the violence they had prepared for others, their "innocent brothers;" the good saved themselves and their own people through their wise advice (16–26). In this catalog, Dhuoda emphasizes the social and political ties which bind a counsellor to those around him and to those who depend upon him. The evil counsellors sought to destroy filial, familial and tribal bonds, in a greedy and envious quest for personal aggrandizement. They suffered justly when they fell, but they brought their families down with them. Doeg and Mordecai, on the other hand, saved others as well as their own people. A kind of *caveat* concludes this catalog, a single sentence and a biblical quotation. God can indeed save even those who have given bad advice, if such willingly repent. It is as if Dhuoda, having drawn up a list of good and bad counsellors, equal numbers on both sides, recognizes that it is impossible for a Christian knight to live his life without ever giving or taking the wrong advice. Living morally in the world of action must include making room for repentance and forgiveness; to live without fault in such a world is simply not possible. These reflections give a sharper edge to her exhortation, in Chapter 11, that William make use of private confession.

CONCLUSION

Has Dhuoda solved the moral dilemma of conflicting loyalties created by the different obligations on which the Frankish world depended? Since she herself sees it as a *practical*, not a *theoretical* problem, she offers no definitive theoretical solution but rather norms and a process for implementing them in the practical, political realm. The first norm to which she holds is that of the primacy of God's claim upon the loyalty of the Christian knight. Of the many obligations that fall upon William, God's is first and, alone, absolute. Obedience to father and lord must be shaped by obedience to the laws of God's kingdom. In such an obedience, due attention must always be paid to keeping both soul and body pure. That phrase returns as almost a refrain through all the chapters of Book III.

Additionally, Dhuoda sees an order of priority among William's various feudal obligations. Among earthly loyalties, William's first duty is to his father, Bernard. Not only is Bernard first in the order of nature (which Dhuoda understands to reflect the divine will), but William's obedience to Charles is contingent upon Bernard's choice of him as sovereign. Practical considerations also support her argument: Bernard is the source of William's rank and his earthly possessions. But Charles' place in his hierarchy of obligations is also a matter of divine command, since all authority comes from God. Dhuoda's view of God's absolute priority is not eschatological. She does not depict the divine commands and the heavenly kingdom as standing over against the world and its political realities. Rather, the divine will is embedded in the social and political structures of the Frankish kingdom. This undoubtedly makes moral decision-making more difficult and more dependent upon spiritual discernment. Therefore, the heart of her solution to the moral dilemma of conflicting obligations is in her exhortation to the formation of conscience and to an ever-deepening spiritual life. Her argument is that such moral and spiritual development will enable William to solve the moral conflicts surrounding the practice of filial and feudal obedience where they truly exist, in the practical order, in the daily life of the Frankish court. What will enable William to negotiate the murky moral waters of his situation is a conscience properly formed and nourished by a mature spiritual life. In Book III of the *Liber Manualis,* Dhuoda describes conscience formation as a process of reading the Scriptures from the perspective of one's concrete situation in life and of understanding one's personal life in scriptural categories. Every chapter is replete with the stories of biblical heroes, held up as models of faith and true obedience. Book III is pervaded by Dhuoda's conviction that the Old Testament, the New Testament and the "present days" form one continuous narrative of salvation. Jewish patriarchs are the "fathers in the faith." The stories of William's personal ancestors, and, by extension, William's own life, continue that history. Therefore, the ancestors in the faith will have faced moral crises similar to William's. His own concrete situation can give him a better understanding of his spiritual ancestors, in bible and family, and he can, with confidence, look to their actions for help in understanding his own.

In the various biblical models which Dhuoda holds up for William's emulation, the discerning reader can find not only the obvious figures but also several ambiguous examples that suggest a modest prophetic voice and an intent at least to challenge if not to subvert the common wisdom of the court. Among the models of filial obedience (III, 3), she places Joseph, a man whose virtue and loyalties were consistently in conflict. A victim of both fraternal envy and of the lust of Potiphar's wife, Joseph survives by his own integrity and his spiritual understanding (demonstrated by his ability to interpret dreams). He rises to power because he is not afraid to give Pharaoh a potentially painful message. He is not above the use of trickery in order to save his family. As a model of obedience, Joseph teaches subtlety, courage and cunning rather than submissiveness. Similarly, in the various lists of exemplary counsellors, Dhuoda names both Daniel (III, 5) and Mordecai (III, 7).[232] Daniel's career as a counselor is long-lasting and fraught with danger at every step. He survives the challenge of Nebuchadnezzar by appealing to the wisdom of his companions and by prayer. To Belshazzar, disclaiming all material rewards though he ultimately receives them, he gives a stark message of moral failure and political defeat. By refusing to abandon his personal, prayerful relationship with the true God of Israel, he defies the edict of Darius and survives the lion's den only through divine intervention. As a counsellor, Daniel is more akin to Nathan, David's prophet, than to the other court counsellors who appear in his story. What he will teach William (if the latter reads the stories as carefully as his mother bids him to) is to reject pragmatism in favor of moral integrity and to tell his lord what is revealed in prayer rather than the triusms of political craftsmanship. Mordecai, not Esther, is the model Dhuoda chooses from the Book of Esther. It is Mordecai who remains faithful to his heritage, who will not take the easy way out that Esther initially offers him, who chastises Esther for forgetting that, despite her prominence, she will not escape the fate of her own people. All three of these biblical figures were in the service of alien kings; each had to be faithful to the true God in the midst of idolatry. Their inclusion suggests that Dhuoda may sniff the evanescent odor of idolatry in the political wisdom of her day. She praises the biblical counsellors for being helpful counsellors "without abandoning their own ways,"[233] underlining the possibility that hers is, in part, a subversive and prophetic message. As a group, William's "ancestors in the faith" will teach him that only fidelity to the law of God, expressed in concrete choices and courageous action, insures a full and final solution to the moral ambiguities of a political theocracy.

---

[232] I am grateful to my colleague, Dr. Daniel Christopher, for calling my attention to the possibilities suggested by Daniel and Mordecai.

[233] ". . . sua non deserentes, utilissimi illi ad consilium fuerent semper" (III, 5, 75–76).

It is, therefore, in the world of action that William's conscience will be truly formed. Ascetical action plays its part. Prayer, almsgiving and the acquisition of virtue, especially the social virtues, are an integral component of the whole process of authentic conscience formation. In acquiring virtue, William must discipline those passions which so often cloud judgment and distort moral perception. Prayer will keep vividly before William's mind the transcendent horizon of God's will and providence against which the true Christian knight can assess the relative moral value of the choices that lie before him. Moral behavior is never a matter of external action only but is also an expression of character which is formed through prayer, the sacraments and the study of the Scripture. But, ultimately, William must be formed in the very practical and social activity which it is his vocation to perform. True morality for one in William's position will be found only in a community of Christian magnates, in the giving and taking of counsel, in decisions made, reviewed and, when necessary, repented. Dhuoda's advice to William is genuine moral theology, not yet neatly and academically distinguished from spirituality, systematic or political theology but made coherent and practical for the world of the court, of the fighting field and of the revolutionary times in which both she and William lived.

APPENDICES

Appendix 1

Dhuoda's Use of the Story of the Syro-Phoenician Woman

Both of us must search for God, my son;
in God's will we take our place, we live, move and have our being.
  Unworthy and insubstantial as a shadow,
    I seek God
        in order to be strong;
  unceasingly
    I ask God's help
        in order to understand.

THIS IS ABSOLUTELY NECESSARY TO ME.

It is not unusual that a troublesome puppy,
under the master's table with the others,
often succeeds in catching and eating the crumbs that fall.
  So powerful, indeed,
  is the one who made the mouth of dumb animals to speak
  and given understanding.

RESPONSORIAL:
The one who prepares a table in the desert
    for those who are faithful followers,
        giving them a satisfying measure of wheat
        in time of need,
    can satisfy my inclination as God's handmaid
        from the divine goodwill.

At least I may be under his table,
    (that is to say, inside holy church),
able to watch, even if from afar, the small dogs there
    (that is, the ministers of his holy altars).

And under that table,

I can collect crumbs of spiritual understanding:
beautiful, lucid and valuable words,
appropriate for both me and you.

I know this because God does not abandon his impoverished ones.

Appendix 2

The Latin text is taken from St. Jerome, *Commentaire sur S. Matthieu*, Emile Bonnard (Ed). Sources Chrétiennes 242 (Paris: Editions du Cerf, 1977): 330–34.

Bk II. On Matthew, Chap 15.

V. 21. Et egressus inde Iesus secessit in partes Tyri et Sidonis.

Scribis et Pharisaeis calumniatoribus derelictis, transgreditur in partes Tyri et Sidonis ut Tyrios Sidioniosque curaret. Mulier autem Cananaea egreditur de finibus pristinis ut clamans filiae impetret sanitatem. Obserua quod in quinto decimo loco filia Cananaea sanetur.

Having left behind the Scribes and Pharisees who calumniated him, Jesus crossed over into the regions of Tyre and Sidon to heal those who lived there. A Canaanite woman left her former borders in order that she might, with her cries, beg him for the health of her daughter. Note that this is the fifteenth healing that takes place [in the narrative].

V. 22. Miserere mei, Domine fili Dauid, filia mea male a daemonio uexatur.

Inde nouit uocare filium Dauid quia egressa iam fuerat de finibus suis et errorem Tyriorum ac Sidoniorum loci ac fidei commutatione dimiserat. **Filia mea male a daemonio uexatur.** Ego filiam ecclesiae puto animas esse credentium quae male a daemonio uexabantur, ignorantes creatorem et adorantes lapidem.

She knew well enough to call him "Son of David" because she had already come out of her borders and changed both her faith and her place by renouncing the errors of Tyre and Sidon. "My daughter is beset by a demonic spirit." I believe that this daughter of the church represents the souls of believers, still ignorant of their creator and adoring stone [idols].

V. 23. Qui non respondit ei uerbum.

Non de superbia pharisaica nec de scribarum supercilio, sed ne ipse sententiae suae uideretur contrarius per quam iusserat: **In uiam gentium ne abieritis et in ciuitates Samaritanorum ne intraueritis (Mt 10:5).** Nolebat enim occasionem calumniatoribus dare, perfectamque salutem gentium passionis et resurrectionis tempori reseruabat.

Not from pharisaic pride nor scribal contempt [does Jesus keep silence] but so that he might not seem to violate his own prescription: **Do not go into the way of the Gentiles and do not enter into the towns of the Samaritans (Mt 10:5)**. He did not wish to give an opportunity to those who wished to calumniate him. He reserved the gift of full salvation for the Gentiles to the time of his passion and resurrection.

Et accedentes discipuli eius rogabant eum dicentes: Dimitte eam quia clamat post nos.

Discipuli illo adhuc tempore mysteria Domini nescientes, uel misericordia commoti, rogabant pro Cananaea muliere (quam alter euangelista Syrophoenissam appellat) uel importunitate eius carere cupientes, quia non ut clementem sed ut durum medicum crebrius inclamaret.

The disciples themselves do not here know the mysteries of the Lord in their proper seasons. They are either moved by compassion or greatly desire to be freed from her insistence, because they intercede for this Canaanite woman—called a Syro-Phoenician by another evangelist—who calls out repeatedly as if she seeks a physician who is not merciful but unfeeling.

V. 24. Non sum missus nisi ad oues perditas domus Israhel.

Non quo et ad gentes non missus sit, sed quo primum ad Israhel missus sit, ut illis non recipientibus euangelium, iusta fieret ad gentes transmigratio. Et significanter dixit: **ad oues perditas domus Israhel** (Cf. Lk 15:4), ut ex hoc loco etiam unam erroneam ouem de alia parabola intellegamus.

Not that he [Jesus] was not sent to the nations but that he was sent first to Israel, so that when they did not receive the gospel he would be justified in turning to the Gentiles. It is significant that he says "to the lost sheep of the house of Israel" so that we may understand here also the one lost sheep of the other parable.

V. 25. At illa uenit et adorauit eum dicens.

Mira sub persona mulieris Cananitidis ecclesiae fides, patientia, humilitas: fides qua credidit sanari posse filiam suam, patientia qua totiens contempta in precibus perseuerat, humilitas qua se non canibus sed catulis comparat. Canes autem ethnici propter idolatriam dicuntur, qui esui sanguinis dediti et cadaueribus mortuorum feruntur in rabiem.

Nota quod ista Cananitis perseueranter primum filium Dauid, deinde
Dominum uocet, et ad extremum adoret ut Deum.

In the person of the Canaanite woman we marvel at the faith, patience, and
humility of the church. She is faithful because she believes that her daughter can
be healed; patient because she perseveres in prayer even while she is being held
in contempt; humble because she compares herself not to dogs, but to little dogs.
The pagan nations are called dogs because of their idolatry; they feed on blood
and dead bodies to the point of madness. Note also that this Canaanite
perseveres from her first insight, in which she calls him "son of David," and then
"Lord," until she finally adores him as God.

**V. 27. At illa dixit: Etiam, Domine, nam et catelli edunt de micis
quae cadunt de mensa dominorum suorum.**

Scio me, inquit, filiorum panem non mereri, nec integros capere posse
cibos, nec sedere ad mensam cum patre, sed contenta sum reliquiis
catulorum, ut per humilitatem micarum ad panis integri ueniam
magnitudinem. O mira rerum conuersio. Israhel quondam filius, nos
canes. Pro diuersitate fidei ordo nominum commutatur. De illis postea
dicitur: **Circumdederunt me canes multi** (Ps 21:17); et: **Videte canes,
uidete malos operarios, uidete concisionem** (Phil 3:2). Nos audimus
cum Syrophoenissa et muliere quae sanguine fluxerat: **Magna est fides
tua, fiat tibi sicut uis** et: **Filia, fides tua te saluam fecit** (Mk 5:34).

I know, she says, that I do not deserve the child's bread, I am unable to grasp
their full nourishment or to sit at the table with the father. I am content with the
left-overs destined for the dogs so that through humility I can finally receive the
full greatness of the bread. What a wondrous turn-about! Israel was once the son
and we, the dogs. Because of a change in faith, the order of the names is
switched. Of the former sons, it would later be said: "A multitude of dogs
surround me" (Ps 21:17) and "avoid the dogs, the evil-doers, the circumcised"
(Phil 3:2). Now in company with the Syrophoenician woman and the woman
with the flow of blood, we [the Gentiles] hear: "Great is your faith, may it be
done to you as you wish" and "Daughter, your faith has saved you" (Mk 5:34).

Appendix 3

Latin text taken from Bede, *In Marci Evangelium Expositio*, D. Hurst (ed). *Corpus Christianorum* 122 (Turnholt: Brepols, 1960): 523-25.

V. 24. Et inde surgens abiit in fines Tyri et Sidonis. Scribis et Pharisaeis calumniatoribus derelictis transgreditur in partes Tyri et Sidonis ut Tyrios Sidoniosque curaret. Et ingressus domum neminem uoluit scire et non potuit latere.

Merito quaeritur quomodo dicatur quia dominus neminem uoluerit iter suum scire nec tamen latere potuerit. Quid enim est quod ille non potuerit qui etiam temporaliter inter homines positus omnia inuisibiliter quae foris agebantur intus cum patre disponebat? Aut quam ob causam putandus est fines Tyri et Sidonis intrasse, nisi ut filiam Syrophoenissae a daemonio liberaret ac per fidem feminae gentilis perfidiam argueret scribarum ac Pharisaeorum? Sed fideliter ac pie sentiendum est quia nequaquam de illo hac in re quod ipse noluit factum est sed fidelibus iter eius sequentibus quid principaliter in bonis quae agunt uelle debeant ostensum. Ingressus quippedomum praecepit discipulis ne se cuiquam in regione ignota quis esset aperirent. At tamen ipse suum illo introitum gentili feminae quibuscumque uoluit ipse prudentibus publicauit ipse cor illius ad quaerendam a se salutem inuisibili accendit instinctu ut exemplo eius discerent quibus sanandi infirmos gratiam conferret in exhibitione miraculorum humani gloriam fauoris quantum possent declinare nec tamen a pio uirtutis opere cessare quando haec fieri uel fides bonorum iuste mereretur uel incredulitas prauorum necessario cogeret. **Et non potuit, inquit, latere.**

Worthily may one inquire why it is said that the Lord wished no one to know of his journey, yet nevertheless it could not be hidden. For what would be impossible for him who even when he was among men in the world, was [still] placed within the Father, invisibly managing all that happened on the outside? What reason must he have had for seeking to go into the borders of Tyre and Sidon, except that he would free the daughter of the Syro-Phoenician woman from a demon and, through the faith of this gentile woman, expose the lack of faith in the scribes and Pharisees? But these things must be grasped with faith and piety: that in no way did anything happen in this matter that he didn't want to happen; that it was shown to those faithfully following his journey what they chiefly ought to desire in the good things that they do. His going into the house certainly showed his disciples that they were not to reveal who he was to anyone in an unknown region. But nevertheless, he himself proclaimed his own entrance to the gentile woman and to whatever prudent person he wanted and he himself inflamed her heart to seek salvation from him by an invisible instinct. [This he did] so that those on whom he confers the grace of healing the sick through the display of miracles might learn by her example how they might avoid the glory of human applause and yet, at the same time, not cease from the piety of good works when such works had to be done, either because the faith of good people deserved them or the unbelief of the vicious necessarily compelled them. "And it could be hidden," he said.

VV. 25–26. Mulier enim statim ut audiuit de eo cuius habebat filia a spiritum immundum intrauit et procidit ad pedes eius; erat autem mulier gentilis Syrophoenissa genere.

Typice autem mulier haec gentilis sed cum fide ad dominum ueniens ecclesiam designat de gentibus collectam. Quae pro filia daemoniaca dominum rogat cum pro populis suis necdum credentibus ut et ipsi a diaboli fraudibus absoluantur supernae pietati supplicat. Quae bene iuxta Matheum de finibus suis egressa in hoc vero euangelista ingressa esse ad dominum atque ad pedes eius procidisse refertur quatenus ex utriusque assertione colligatur quod illi solum fideliter ac recte pro errantibus orant qui priscas suae perfidiae mansiones relinquunt atque in domum domini uidelicet ecclesiam pia se deuotione transferunt.

This Gentile woman who comes with faith to the Lord is a type of the Church which is gathered from the nations. When she beseeched the Lord, in her piety, on behalf of her possessed daughter, she was, in fact, interceding with Him for her people—not yet believers—that they might be set free from the devil's delusions. She was a bearer of good news—in very truth an evangelist. The account in Matthew tells us that she left behind her own borders in order to come to the Lord and did not stop until she came right up to his feet. From her story we may see what it takes to pray properly and faithfully for those in error; it requires that true believers abandon their earlier dwellings, homes of faithlessness that no longer shelter them properly, and move with pious devotion into the House of the Lord, that is the Church.

VV. 26–27. Et rogabat, inquit, eum ut daemonium eiceret de filia eius. Qui dixit illi: Sine prius saturari filios.

Quasi apertius diceret, Restat futurum ut etiam uos qui de gentibus estis salutem consequamini, sed primo oportet Iudaeos qui merito antiquae electionis filiorums Dei solent nomine censeri pane caeli refici et sic tandem gentibus uitae pabula ministrari.

The Lord tells this woman that the children of the household must be fed first. He seems to say openly that there will come a future time when you who are from pagan nations will attain salvation. But first it belongs to the Jews by right of the ancient election; they are to continue to be esteemed sons of God, refreshed by the bread of heaven, until such time as the food of life will be distributed to the gentiles.

VV. 27–28. Non est enim bonum sumere panem filiorum et mittere canibus. At illa respondit et dicit ei: Vtique, domine, nam et catelli comedunt de micis puerorum.

[Mira sub persona mulieris Cananitidis ecclesiae fides patientia humilitas praedicatur fides qua crediderit sanari posse filiam suam patientia qua toties contempta ut Matheus scribit in precibus perseuerat humilitas qua se non canibus sed catulis comparat. Scio me, inquit, filiorum panem non mereri nec integros capere posse cibos nec sedere ad mensam cum patre sed contenta sum reliquiis catulorum ut humilitate micarum ad panis integri ueniam magnitudinem. Mira rerum conuersio Israhel quondam filius nos canes pro diuersitate fidei ordo nominum commutatur. De illis postea dicitur: Circumdederunt me canes multi; et: Videte canes uidete malos operarios uidete concisionem.] Taken from Jerome.

[In the person of the Canaanite woman we admire the faith, patience, and humility of the church. She is faithful because she believes that her daughter can be healed; patient because she perseveres in prayer even while she is being held in contempt; humble because she compares herself not to dogs, but to little dogs. I know, she says, that I do not deserve the children's bread, I am unable to grasp their full nourishment or to sit at the table with the father. I am content with the left-overs destined for the dogs so that through humility I can finally receive the full greatness of the bread. What a wondrous turn-about! Israel was once the son and we, the dogs. Because of a change in faith, the order of the names is switched. Of the former sons, it would later be said: "A multitude of dogs surround me" (Ps 21:17) and "avoid the dogs, the evil-doers, the circumcised" (Phil 3:2)].

De nobis a latratu blasphemiae contradictionis ad pietatis gratiam conuersis ipse alibi dicit: **Et alias oues habeo quae non sunt ex hoc ouili, et illas oportet me adducere, et uocem meam audient.** Notandum sane quod mystice loquitur credens ex gentibus mulier quia catelli sub mensa comedunt de micis puerorum. Mensa quippe est scriptura sancta quae nobis panem uitae ministrat. Hinc etenim dicit ecclesia: **Parasti in conspectu meo mensam aduersus eos qui**

tribulant me. Micae puerorum interna sunt mysteria scripturarum quibus humilium solent corda refici de quibus alias sanctae ecclesiae promittitur dicente propheta de domino: **Qui posuit fines tuos pacem et adipe frumenti satians te.** Non ergo crustas sed micas de pane puerorum edunt catelli quia conueris ad fidem qui erant despecti in gentibus non litterae superficiem in scripturis sed spiritalium medullam sensuum qua in bonis actibus proficere ualeant inquirunt. Et hoc sub mensa dominorum dum uerbis sacri eloquii humiliter subditi ad implenda quae praecepta sunt cuncta sui cordis et corporis officia subponunt quatenus ad speranda quae a domino promissa sunt praemia in caelis merito se debitae humilitatis erigant.

Those of us who are newly converted are dogs indeed whose contrary and blasphemous barking has been transformed into gracious and pious speech. Elsewhere the Lord has spoken about us more gently: "Other sheep I have which are not of this fold; I will call them forth and they will hear my voice" (Jn 10:16). When the Gentile woman of faith speaks of the dogs under the table who eat the children's left-over crumbs, we must interpret her words in a mystical way. The table is Holy Scripture which serves us the bread of life. The church says it this way: "You have prepared a table for me in the sight of my enemies" (Ps 22:5). The crumbs left by the children are the inner mysteries of the Scriptures by which the humble are accustomed to refresh their hearts. This is the way Holy Church interprets the promise made by the prophet of the Lord in another part of the Scriptures: "The one who made peace within your borders has filled you with the marrow of wheat" (Ps 147:14). As it turns out, then, the dogs end up eating, not the crusts but the crumbs of bread. When those who were once looked upon with contempt because they were gentiles are finally converted to the faith, they begin to study, not the superficial letter of the Scripture [crusts] but the very marrow of its spiritual sense [crumbs], hoping to gain an advantage through good deeds. That is why they humbly place themselves under the table of their hosts; they replace the eloquence of holy words by the accomplishment of every duty that has been commanded. By this humility of heart and obedience of body they hope to rise up to the heavenly rewards promised by the Lord.

V. 29. Et ait illi: Propter hunc sermonem uade, exiit daemonium de filia tua.

Propter humilem matris fidelemque sermonem filiam deseruit daemonium. Vbi datur exemplum cathecizandi et baptizandi infantes quia uidelicet per fidem et confessionem parentum in baptismo liberantur a diabolo paruuli qui necdum per se sapere uel aliquid agere boni possunt aut mali.

154 DHUODA: NINTH CENTURY MOTHER & THEOLOGIAN

As regards the final verse of this story, the Scriptures say that because of the faithful words of this humble mother, the demon abandoned the daughter. This teaches us a lesson about the catechizing and baptizing of infants: through the faith and confession of the parents in baptism, small children may be freed from the devil's control. On their own or by the work of another, they can discern between good and evil and act upon their discernment.

Appendix 4

Outline of Dhuoda's Treatment of Moral Development

Books IV-VI of the Liber Manualis

Book IV:
Chaps 1–3: The general principle of moral development: to practice the particular virtues which opose the dangerous vices. The examples of envy and pride.
Chaps 4–7: The practice of the gifts of the Holy Spirit, compared to the military exercises of the Christian knight. The gifts enable the Christian to build a strong wall against encircling vices.
Chap 8: The active reading of the eight beatitudes are a battle against vice.
Chap 9, Coda: The Christian Knight should aid the poor.

Book V:
Nine chapters on temptations and tribulations as part of the general struggle against the vices.

Book VI:
Chap 1: The gifts of the Holy Spirit together with the beatitudes constitute a full program for moral growth.
Chap 2–3: Admonitions on the need to seek perfection.
Chap 4: The moral development of the Christian is an ascent of the fifteen steps formed by the gifts and beatitudes.

Appendix 5

Structure of Dhuoda's Explanation of Beatitudes

ADMONITION   leads up to   *QUOTE OF BEATITUDE*
Be patient (do not act in anger). . .   "Blessed are the peacemakers"
Be meek (cultivate good works). . .   "Blessed are the meek"
If you meet a helpless person. . .

EXCURSUS
Lengthy disquisition on the importance of the poor
TRANSITION: "Blessed is the one who fears the Lord"

Love purity (love purity). . .   "Blessed are the pure in heart"
Love the poor (conceal rank). . .   "Blessed are the poor in spirit"
Love justice (do justice in the courts). . .

EXCURSUS
Lengthy treatment of justice...
"Blessed are those who hunger and thirst for justice"
Be merciful (seek mercy in legal action). . .   "Blessed are the merciful"
Be meek (use gentleness in all action). . .   "Blessed are the meek"
Be generous (give all you can). . .
"Blessed are those who think of the poor"

CODA
Shorter disquisition on almsgiving.

SELECTED BIBLIOGRAPHY

Primary Sources

Alcuin. *De Virtutibus et Vitiis*, *PL*, vol. 101.

Ambrose. *De Spiritu Sancto*, *PL* vol. 16.

Augustine. *De Sermone Domini in Monte Secundum Matthaeum Libri Duo*, *PL*, vol. 34.

Augustine. "On Christian Instruction." In *Writings of Saint Augustine*, *Fathers of the Church Series*, vol. 4, translated by John J. Gavigan. New York: Cima Publishing, 1947.

Augustine. *The Lord's Sermon on the Mount*. *ACW*, vol. 5, translated by John J. Jepson. Westminster, MD: Newman Press, 1956.

Augustine. *Sermo 347*, *PL*, vol. 139.

Augustine. *Sermons on New Testament Lessons*. *NPNF*, vol. 6, translated by R. G. MacMullen.

Bede. *In Marci Evangelium Exposito*. *CC*, vol. 120, edited by D. Hurst.Turnholt: Brepols, 1960.

Benedict. *The Rule*. Translated by Anthony C. Meisel and M.L. del Mastro. Garden City, NJ: Doubleday & Co., 1975.

Carolingian Chronicles. Translated by Bernard Walter Scholz with Barbara Rogers. Ann Arbor: University of Michigan Press, 1970.

Chrysostom, John. *Homily XXIV*. *NPNF*, vol. 13, translated by G. Alexander. Grand Rapids, MI: Eerdmans Publishing Co, 1969.

Chrysostom, John. *Homily XXII on St. John*. *NPNF*, vol. 14, translated by Phillip Schaffin. Grand Rapids, MI: Eerdmans Publishing Co, 1975.

Dhuoda. *Manuel pour mon fils*. *SC*, vol. 225, edited by Pierre Riché. Paris: Editions du Cerf, 1975.

Dhouda. *Handbook for William: A Carolingian Woman's Counsel for Her Son*. Translated by Carol Neel. Lincoln and London: University of Nebraska Press, 1991.

Dhouda. *The Liber Manualis of Dhuoda: Advice of a Ninth-Century Mother for Her Son*. Translated by Myra E. Bowers. Ph.D. diss., Catholic University, 1977.

Jerome. *Commentary on St. Matthew*. *SC*, vols. 242 and 243, edited by Emile Bonnard. Paris: Editions du Cerf, 1977, 1978.

Origen. *Commentary on John*. *ANF*, vol. 10, translated by John Patrick. Grand Rapids, MI: Eerdmans Publishing Co., 1975.

Von Reims, Hinkmar. *De Ordine palatii.* Edited by Thomas Grass and Rudolf Schieffer. Hannover, 1980.

Secondary Sources

Albousse, Lionel. *Histoire de la ville d'Uzès.* Uzès, 1903.

Baldovin, John. *The Urban Character of Christian Worship.* Orientalia Christiana Analecta, vol. 228. Rome: Pon. Institutum Studiorum Orientalium, 1987.

Barre, Henri. *Les Homéliares Carolingiens de L'école d'Auxerre*, Studi E Testi, vol. 225. Vatican City: Biblioteca Apostolica Vaticana, 1962.

Barre, Henri. "L'Homéliaire Carolingien de Mondsee," *RB* 71 (1961): 75.

Beissel, Stephen. S.J. *Entstehung der Perikipen des Romischen Messbuches.* Freiburg: Herdersche Verlagshandlung, 1907.

Benoit, F., et al. *Villes épiscopales de Provence.* Paris, 1954.

Beraud, Pierre. *Uzès, son diocèse, son histoire.* Uzès: Editions de la Cigâle, 1947.

Bernstein, Richard J., *Beyond Objectivism and Relativism: Science, Hermeneutics and Praxis.* Phila: University of Pennsylvania Press, 1983.

Bessmertny, Y. "Le monde vu par une femme noble au Ixè siècle: La perception du monde dans l'aristocratie carolingienne," *Moyen Age* 93 (1987): 162–84.

Bloomfield, Morton W. *The Seven Deadly Sins.* Michigan: State College Press, 1952.

Bouchard, Constance. "Family Structure and Family Consciousness among the Aristocracy in the Ninth to Eleventh Centuries," *Francia* 14 (1986): 639–58.

Bouyer, Louis. *Bible and Liturgy.* Notre Dame, IN: University of Notre Dame Press, 1964.

Bradley, Ritamary. "Backgrounds of the Title *Speculum* in Medieval Literature," *Speculum* 29 (1954): 100–15.

Bradshaw, Paul F. "The Use of the Bible in Liturgy: Some Historical Perspectives," *Studia Liturgica* 22 (1992): 35–52.

Burghhardt, Walter J. "On Early Christian Exegesis," *TS*, vol. 11 (1950): 78–116.

Burton-Christie, Douglas. *The Word in the Desert: Scripture and Quest for Holiness in Early Christian Monasticism.* New York and Oxford: Oxford University Press, 1993.

Busquet, Raoul, et al. *Histoire de la provence.* Paris, 1972.

Cabaniss, Allen. *Son of Charlemagne: A Contemporary Life of Louis the Pious.* Syracuse, SUNY Press, 1961.

Calmette, J. *De Bernard, Sancti Wilhelmi filio.* Toulouse, 1902.

Cantelli, Silvia. *Angelomo e La Scuola Esegetica Di Luxeuil I.* Spoleto: Centro di Studi Sull' Alto Medioevo, 1990.

Catry, Patrick. "Lire l'écriture selon Saint Grégoire le Grand," *Collectanea Cisterciensa* 34 (1972): 177–201.

Cazier, Pierre. "Le Livre des Règles de Tyconius," *REAug* 19 (1973): 241–61.

Chalon, Michel. "L'inscription juive de Narbonne et la condition des Juifs en Narbonne á la fin du VIIè siècle," *Hommage a Andre Dupont.* Montpellier, 1974.

Chélini, Madame J. *Le Vocabulaire Politique et Social dans la Correspondance d'Alcuin.* Nazareth, Aix-en Provence: La Pensée Universitaire, 1959.

Clark, Elizabeth. *Women in the Early Church.* Wilmington, DE: Glazier, 1983.

Claussen, M.A.. "God and Man in Dhuoda's *Liber Manualis.*" In *Women in the Church, SCH* vol. 27, edited by W.J. Sheils and Diana Wood. Oxford: Blackwell, 1990.

Clayton, Mary. *The Cult of the Virgin Mary in Anglo Saxon England.* Cambridge: The University Press, 1990.

Contreni, John J. "Carolingian Biblical Studies." In *Carolingian Essays*, edited by Uta-Renate Blumenthal. Washington, DC: The Catholic University of America Press, 1983.

Contreni, John J. "Inharmonius Harmony: Education in the Carolingian World," *Annals of Scholarship*, vol. 1 (1980): 81–96.

Cuvillier, Jean-Pierre. *L'Allemagne Médiévale.* Paris, 1979.

Danielou, Jean. *The Bible and the Liturgy.* Notre Dame, IN: University of Notre Dame Press, 1956.

De Blic, J. "Pour l'histoire de la théologie des dons," *RAM*, vol. 22 (1955): 117–79.

De Lubac, Henri. *Exégèse Médiévale: Les quatre sens de l'écriture.* Lyons: Aubier, 1959–1962.

De Nostradamus, Caesar. *L'Histoire et Chronique de Province.* Lyons, 1614.

De Urbel, Fray Justo Perez, et al. *Liber Commicus*, Edicion Critica, Serie Liturgica, vols. II and III. Madrid, 1950.

Dronke, Peter. *Women Writers of the Middle Ages.* Cambridge: Cambridge University Press, 1984.

Dupont, A. *Quelques aspects de la vie rurale en Septimanie Carolingienne.* Montpellier, 1954.

Dupont, A. "Uzès pendant le period du haut Moyen Age," *École Antique de Nîmes*, 21 Session, 1940.

Ebeling, Gerhard. *Word and Faith.* Philadelphia: Fortress Press, 1963.

Freed, John B. "Reflections on the Medieval German Nobility," *American Historical Review* 91 (1986): 553–75.

160 DHUODA: NINTH CENTURY MOTHER & THEOLOGIAN

Frere, Walter. *Studies in Early Roman Liturgy II: The Roman Gospel Lectionary*, Alcuin Club Collections, vol. 30. London: Oxford University Press, 1934.

Frere, Walter H. *Studies in Early Roman Liturgy III: The Roman Epistle-Lectionary*, Alcuin Club Collections, vol. 32. Oxford, 1935.

Gamber, Klaus. *Codices liturgici latini antiquiores*. Fribourg, 1963-1968.

Gamber, Klaus. *Missa Romensis, Beitrage zur fruhen romischen Liturgie und zu Anfangen des Missals Romanum*, Studia Patristica et Liturgica, vol. 3. Regensburg: Pustet, 1970.

Gatch, Milton McC.. "Carolingian Preaching." In *Preaching and Theology in Anglo-Saxon England: Ælfric and Wulfstan*. Toronto and Buffalo: University of Toronto Press, 1977.

Grégoire, Reginald. *Les Homéliares du moyen âge*, Rerum Ecclesiasticarum Documenta, Series Maior, Fontes VI. Rome: Herder, 1966.

Gryson, Roger. *The Ministry of Women in the Early Church*. Translated by Jean LaPorte and Mary Louise Hall. Collegeville, MN: Liturgical Press, 1980.

Guzie, Tad W. "Patristic Hermeneutics," *TS* 32 (December, 1971): 647-58.

Head, Thomas, "Carolingian Bishops." PAPER presented at the 26th International Congress of Medieval Studies, Kalamazoo, MI, May, 1991.

Hennebicque, Regine. "Structures familiales et politiques au IXè siècle," *Révue Historique* 265 (1981): 289-90.

Herlihy, David. "Land, Family, and Women in Continental Europe, 701-1200," *Traditio* 18 (1962): 89-120.

Hildgarth, Jocelyn N. *Isidoriana*. Edited by Manuel C. Diaz y Diaz. Leon: Centro de Estudios San Isidoro, 1961.

Horsley, G.H.R. *New Documents Illustrating Early Christianity*. Macquarrie University: The Ancient History Documentary Research Centre, 1987.

Jungmann, Josef. *The Mass of the Roman Rite: Its Origins and Development*. 2 vols. New York: Benziger Bros., 1951.

Kannengiesser, Charles. *Le Bible de tous les temps*. 4 vols. Paris: Beauchesne, 1984-1985.

Kelly, J.N.D.. *Jerome: His Life, Writings and Controversies*. San Francisco: Harper and Row, 1975.

Klauser, Theodore. *Das Romische Capitulare Evangeliorum*. Munster, 1935.

Laistner, M.L.W. "A Ninth-Century Commentator on the Gospel according to Matthew," *Harvard Theological Review* 20 (1927): 129-49.

Lampe, G. W. H. "The Reasonableness of Typology." In *Essays on Typology*. London: SCM Press LTD, 1956.

Leclerq, Jean. "Le IIIè livre de Homélies de Bede le Vénérable," *RecTh* 14 (1947): 211-18.

Leclerq, Jean. *The Love of Learning and the Desire for God: A Study of Monastic Culture.* Translated by Catharine Misrashi. New York: Fordham University Press, 1961.

Lewis, Archibald. *The Development of Southern French and Catalan Society.* Austin, TX: University of Texas Press, 1965.

Lofstedt, Bengt. "Zu Dhoudas Liber Manualis," *Arctos* 15 (1981): 67–83.

Lot, Ferdinand, et al. *Histoire du Moyen Age, I.* Paris, 1928.

MacHaffie, Barbara J. *Her Story: Women in Christian Tradition.* Philadelphia: Fortress Press, 1986.

Maddox, Randy L. "The Recovery of Theology as a Practical Discipline," *TS* 51 (1990): 650–72.

Martin, Lawrence T. "The Two Worlds in Bede's Homilies: The Biblical Event and the Listeners' Experience." In *Preacher and Word in the Middle Ages*, edited by Thomas L. Amos, Eugene A. Green and Beverly Mayne Kienzle. Kalamazoo, MI: Medieval Institute Publications, 1989.

Mayeski, Marie Anne. *Women: Models of Liberation.* Kansas City, MO: Sheed and Ward, 1989.

McKitterick, Rosamund. *The Carolingians and the Written Word.* New York and Cambridge: Cambridge University Press, 1989.

McKitterick, Rosamund. *The Frankish Kingdoms under the Carolingians 751–987.* New York: Longmans, 1983.

McNally, Robert E. *The Bible in the Early Middle Ages.* Westminster, MD: The Newman Press, 1959.

McNally, Robert E. "Notes on Medieval Exegesis," *TS* 22 (1961): 445–54.

Morin, D.G.. "Le plus ancien *Comes* où Lectionnaire de l'église Romaine," *RB* 27 (1910).

Murphy, Roland E. "Patristic and Medieval Exegesis—Help or Hindrance," *The Catholic Biblical Quarterly* 43 (Oct. 1981): 505–16.

Nelson, Janet L. "National Synods, Kingship as Office, and Royal Anointing: An Early Medieval Syndrome," *SCH*, vol. 7. Oxford: Basil Blackwell, 1971.

Nelson, Janet L. "Les femmes et l'évangelisation au Ixè siècle." Révue du Nord 68 (1986): 471–85.

Ong, Walter J. "Orality, Literacy, and Medieval Textualization," *New Literary History XVI* (1984–85): 1–13.

Orlandis, Jose. "Bible et Royauté dans les Conciles de l'Espagne wisigotho-catholique," *Annuarium Historia Conciliarum* (1986): 51–57.

Poulin, Joseph-Claude. *L'Idéal de Sainteté dans L'Aquitaine Carolingienne.* Quebec: Les Presses de L'Université Laval, 1975.

Riché, Pierre. *Daily Living in the World of Charlemagne.* Philadelphia: University of Pennsylvania Press, 1978.

Riché, Pierre (Ed). "Instruments de travail et méthodes de l'exégete a l'époque carolingienne," *Le Moyen Age et la Bible*. Vol. 4, *Bible de tous les Temps*, edited by Charles Kannengiesser. Paris: Beauchesne, 1984.

Riché, Pierre. "L'Enseignement et la culture des Laïcs dans l'occident pre-carolingien," *Settimane* 19 (1971): 231–253.

Riché, Pierre. *L'Hagiographie, cultures and sociétés*. Paris: 1981.

Riché, Pierre. "Les Bibliothèques de trois aristocrates laïcs carolingiens," *Le Moyen Age* 69 (1963): 87–104.

Ricoeur, Paul. "The Model of the Text: Meaningful Action Considered as a Text." In *Hermeneutics and the Human Sciences*, edited and translated by J. Thompson. Cambridge: Cambridge University Press, 1981.

Ringe, Sharon. "A Gentile Woman's Story." In *Feminist Interpretation of the Bible*, edited by L.M. Russell. Oxford: Blackwell, 1985.

Salmon, Pierre. *Le Lectionnaire de Luxeuil, Édition et Étude Comparative*. Collectanea Biblica Latina, Vol VII. Vatican City: Libreria Vaticana, 1944.

Schneiders, Sandra M. *The Revelatory Text*. San Francisco: Harper, 1991, 21–25.

Simonetti, Manlio. *Profilo Storico dell'exegesi Patristica*. Sussidi Patristica 1. Rome: Istituto Patristico Augustinianum, 1981.

Smalley, Beryl. *The Study of the Bible in the Middle Ages*. 2d ed. Notre Dame, IN: University of Notre Dame Press, 1964.

Smetana, Cyril L. "Aelfric and the Early Medieval Homiliary," *Traditio* 15 (1959): 163–204.

Smith, C.T. *Historical Geography of Western Europe*. New York: Praeger, 1967.

Smith, Julia. "The Cult of the Holy." PAPER presented at the 26th International Congress of Medieval Studies, Kalamazoo, MI, May, 1991.

Sot, Michel. "Spiritualité et Sainteté chez les grandes laïcs carolingians," *Revue d'Histoire de la spiritualité* 52 (1976): 295-302.

Spicq, C. *Esquisse d'une histoire de l'exégèse latine au moyen âge*. Paris, 1944.

Stegmuller, Friedrich. *Reportorium biblicum Medii Aevi*. Madrid, 1950-1981.

Steinmetz, David C. "The Superiority of Pre-Critical Exegesis," *Theology Today* 37 (1980): 27–38.

Sullivan, Richard E. "The Carolingian Age: Reflections on Its Place in the History of the Middle Ages," *Speculum* 64 (1989): 267–306.

Thouzard, J. "Isaie XI, 2-3 et les sept dons du S. Esprit," *RB* VIII (1899): 249–66.

Tracy, David. *The Analogical Imagination: Christian Theology and the Culture of Pluralism*. New York: Crossroads, 1986.

Vogel, Cyrille. *Introduction aux sources de l'histoire de culte chrétien au moyen age.* Spoleto: Centro italiano di studi sull'alto medioevo, 1964.

Wallace-Hadrill, J.M. *Early Medieval History.* New York: Barnes and Noble, 1975.

Wallace-Hadrill, J.M. *The Frankish Church.* Oxford: Clarendon Press, 1983.

Wallace-Hadrill, J.M. and R.H.C. Davis. "History in the Mind of Archbishop Hincmar." In *The Writing of History in the Middle Ages.* Oxford: Clarendon Press, 1981.

Walsh, Katherine and Diana Wood (Eds). *The Bible in the Medieval World.* Oxford: Basil Blackwell, 1985.

Wemple, Suzanne. *Women in Frankish Society.* Philadelphia: University of Pennsylvania Press, 1984.

Whiting, C.E. "The Life of the Venerable Bede." In *Bede: His Life, Times, and Writings*, edited by A. Hamilton Thompson. New York: Russell and Russell, 1966.

Willis, G.G. *St. Augustine's Lectionary.* Alcuin Club Collections, vol. 44. London, 1962.

Wilmart, Dom Andre. "Le *Comes* de Murbach," *RB* 30 (1913): 25–69.

Wilmart, Dom Andre. "Le Lectionnaire d'Alcuin," *Ephem Lit* 2 (1937): 136–97.

Wollasch, Joachim. "Eine adlige Familie des fruhen Mittlealters: Ihr Selbstandnis und ihre Wirklichheit," *Archiv fur Kulturgeschichte* 39 (1957): 150–88.

Woollcombe, K. J.. "The Biblical Origens and Patristic Development of Typology." In *Essays on Typology.* London: SCM Press LTD, 1956.

INDICES

PROPER NAMES INDEX

Aaron 46
Abner 125
Abraham 55, 125, 127
Absalom 123, 139
Achior 137
Achitophel 139
Adam 48, 113
Aelfric 75, 162
Agimond 33
Ahasuerus 139
Alaric 76
Alcuin 3, 31, 32, 39, 47, 96-97,
    157, 159, 160, 163
Aldhelm of Malmesbury 96
Ambrose 31, 32, 42, 108, 157
Aquinas 2, 7
Athanasius 32, 41
Augustine 3, 31, 32, 41, 42, 45,
    47, 48, 51, 60, 66,
    69-71, 82, 87, 93, 94,
    101-106, 108, 116, 122,
    129, 157, 163
Baldovin, John 158
Barthes, Roland 41
Basil 32, 161, 163
Bede 32, 41-44, 66, 68, 74, 75,
    80-87, 89-92, 150, 157,
    160, 161, 163
Belshazzar 137, 143
Benedict 16, 31, 100, 108, 137,
    157
Benoit, F. 158
Bernard 9-13, 35, 60, 114, 117,
    120, 121, 125, 141, 157,
    158
Bertha, Queen of Kent 82
Bessmertny, Y. 158
Bloomfield, Morton W. 158
Bourrilly 15
Bradshaw, Paul F. 158

Burton-Christie, Douglas 41, 52,
    53
Busquet, Raoul 158
Calmette, J. 158
Calvin 122
Cassian 32, 95
Cassiodorus 32
Catry, Patrick 159
Cazier, Pierre 159
Charlemagne 10, 11, 18, 33, 37,
    39, 75, 158, 161
Charles 12, 15, 16, 37, 61, 117,
    118, 124, 125, 127, 141,
    160, 162
Chélini, Madame J. 159
Childebert, the King of the Franks
    19
Claussen, M.A. 159
Clement 67
Contreni, John J. 159
Count of Barcelona 10
Cyprian 32
Daniel 7, 97, 137, 144
Darius 143
David 3, 41, 68, 125, 127, 139,
    143, 147, 149, 160, 162
de Blic, J. 159
De Nostradamus, Caesar 159
De Urbel, Fray Justo Perez 159
Dhuoda 5, 4-9, 10-13, 17-32,
    34-39, 41, 43-48, 51-63,
    65-70, 72, 74, 75, 82,
    85-92, 94-101, 104-139,
    141-145, 155, 156, 157,
    160
Doeg the Edomite 139
Ebeling, Gerhard 159
Eco, Umberto 41
Esther 139, 143
Ethelbert 82
Eusebius of Cremona 75
Freed, John B. 159

Frere, Walter H. 160
Gottshalk 37
Gregory the Great 29, 31, 32, 41, 43, 48, 68, 95, 112
Guarnarius 21
Guzie, Tad W. 160
Haman 139
Heli 123
Heliodorus 76
Hennebicque, Regine 160
Herlihy, David 160
Hildgarth, Jocelyn N. 160
Hincmar 37, 39, 48, 54, 133, 134, 157, 163
Holofernes 137
Homer 44
Horsley, G.H.R. 160
Irenaeus 41, 42, 57
Isaac 8, 123, 125, 127
Isaiah 101, 102
Isidore of Seville 29, 31, 32, 47, 131, 137
Jacob 8, 123, 127
Jepson, John J. 101-104, 157
Jerome 32, 41, 42, 66, 72, 74-84, 86, 87, 92, 101, 147, 152, 157
Jesus 49, 73, 74, 77-81, 83, 86, 122, 147, 148
Joab 125
Job 57, 114
John the Baptist 13
Jonathan 127
Joseph 99, 123, 137, 143, 144, 162
Judith 11
Julian of Norwich 57
Julian of Toledo 32
Jungmann, Josef 160
Kannengiesser, Charles 160
Klauser, Theodore 67, 160
Lewis, Archibald 161
Lofstedt, Bengt 161

Louis the Pious 10-12, 21, 61, 117, 121, 127, 128, 135
Louis, the king of Aquitaine 10
Mabillon 35
MacHaffie, Barbara J. 161
Mark 74, 80, 107
Martin, Lawrence T. 161
Matthew 72, 74, 75, 126, 147, 151, 157, 160
Mayeski, Marie Anne 161
McNally, Robert E. 161
Migne 137
Mordecai 143
Morin, D.G. 161
Moses 98, 99, 115, 137
Nathan 141
Nebuchadnezzar 137, 143
Nelson, Janet L. 161
Nepotian 77
Nithard 11, 12, 133
Noah 44
Ong, Walter J. 161
Origen 32, 43, 49, 66, 67, 72-74, 75, 80, 158
Orlandis, Jose 161
Paul 24-27, 33, 41, 43, 49, 52, 57, 58, 75, 97, 107, 128, 130, 138, 158
Paul the Deacon 33, 75
Pauline 46, 136
Pepin II 12
Peter 4, 9, 35, 62, 159
Philo 45, 67
Potiphar 97, 142
Potiphar's wife 97, 142
Poulin, Joseph-Claude 161
Primasius 32
Prosper 32, 128
Prudence 31, 96, 124, 126, 134, 138
Ps-Cyprien 131
Ratramnus of Corbie 37
Rebeccah 8

Rhabanus 34, 91, 121
Roman Empire 13-15, 18, 19
Salmon, Pierre 162
Samuel 137, 139
Sem 123
Simonetti, Manlio 162
Sirach 115, 120, 122
Smalley, Beryl 162
Smaragdus 75, 135
Smetana, Cyril L. 162
Smith, C.T. 162
Sot, Michel 162
Stegmuller, Friedrich 162
Steinmetz, David C. 162
Susanna 97

Thouzard, J. 162
Vogel, Cyrille 162
Wala 11
Walsh, Katherine 163
Whiting, C.E. 163
Wido 95, 116
William 8-12, 21, 23-29, 35, 38, 48, 49, 51-56, 58-61, 63, 87, 91, 93-100, 105, 107-115, 117-122, 124-133, 136-144
Wilmart, Dom André 163
Woollcombe, K. J. 163

TOPICAL INDEX

abbot(s) 6, 39, 55, 100, 116, 135
action(s) 1, 25, 50, 52, 53, 54,
    55, 60, 61, 69, 76, 77,
    81, 98, 106, 107, 108,
    110, 115, 117, 118, 129,
    136, 141, 142, 144, 156
active life 39, 104
Adam 48, 113
Adam and Eve 113
adolescent 6, 99
adversity 106
affection 26, 59, 79, 127, 129
allegiance 117, 121, 129
allegory(ies) 5, 40, 43-45, 47,
    75, 82, 86, 129
almoners 132
almsgiving 115, 144, 156
altar(s) 66, 89, 91, 131, 145
ambiguity(ies) 73, 105, 117, 118,
    121, 126, 144
ambition 121, 122
analogy 59
ancestors, ancestry 18, 28, 38,
    48, 107, 124, 125, 126,
    137, 142, 146
angelic 48, 97
anger 94, 96-98, 116, 139, 156
animal(s) 58, 76, 90, 96, 129,
    145
annals 30, 48, 159
anointed 132
anthropology, anthropological
    64, 101, 103
antithesis 72, 73, 75, 79, 80, 83,
    84, 86, 90
Apostle(s) 42, 78, 79, 83,
    130
aristocracy 11, 30, 32, 113, 132,
    158
artisan(s) 18, 135, 136, 138

ascetical 40, 62, 63, 101, 105,
    118, 144
audience(s) 1, 4, 6, 23, 69, 87,
    89, 116
authority(ies) 7, 10, 14, 15, 21,
    24, 25, 27, 39, 86, 114,
    117, 118, 121, 132, 134,
    141
banquet table 111
baptism, baptismal 13, 25, 44,
    85, 86, 154
barbarian(s) 14, 15, 42, 76, 77
battle 12, 60, 100, 104, 116, 120,
    155
beatitude of mercy 103
beatitude(s) 5, 6, 26, 55, 93-95,
    97, 99-109, 111-113,
    115, 116, 136, 155, 156
Benedictine 3, 16, 74, 100
bible 1, 3, 5, 39, 43, 47, 49, 50,
    54, 65, 67, 72, 77, 142,
    158, 160-163
biblical interpretation 4, 6, 8, 41,
    55, 65
biblical models 121, 123, 125,
    127, 128, 139, 142
biblical theology 7, 38, 43, 44
birth 20, 21, 25, 26, 46, 96, 121
bishop(s) 1, 6, 9, 14-16, 18,
    19, 39, 54, 55, 62,
    69, 80, 116, 135
blessing(s) 8, 46, 58, 111,
    123, 125, 126, 129
book(s) 3, 6, 8, 10, 17-19, 21,
    23-25, 27-33, 34,
    35, 45, 46, 48, 49,
    51, 52, 53, 54, 56-58,
    61, 63, 66, 69, 70, 81,
    86-88, 91, 93, 94, 96,
    99, 100, 105, 108, 114,
    117-124, 127-130,
    132, 134, 136, 139,

141-143, 155
border(s) 13, 17, 73, 76, 81, 84,
    147, 150, 151, 153
bread 60, 66, 67, 73, 76, 78-80,
    84, 85, 89, 90, 111, 131,
    149, 152, 154
bread and wine 131
business dealing 111
calumny 77, 78
canon 18, 70
canticle(s) 46, 68
Carolingian theology 37, 38
catalog(s) 30, 32, 66, 74, 93-95,
    99, 116, 123, 139
catalog of vices 93, 99
character(s) 2, 4, 8, 18, 25, 28,
    34, 42, 47, 55, 79, 86,
    120, 124, 131, 132, 135,
    144, 158
charity 53, 60, 127
chastity 97, 98 127
chiasmus 79
chrism 131
Christ(s) 40, 44, 49, 63, 67,
    83, 101, 115, 128,
    129, 131, 136
Christian 22, 25, 26, 28, 37, 38
    40, 41, 44, 45, 48-50,
    55-61, 63, 65, 70, 82,
    83, 85, 86, 88, 93, 94,
    95, 100-107, 109, 111,
    113, 115-118, 121, 128,
    134, 135, 137, 141, 142,
    144, 155, 158, 161
Christian life 38, 41, 50, 59-61,
    70, 88, 100, 102-105,
    118, 137
christological 49, 63, 101, 129
chronicles 10-12, 48, 157
church 3, 9, 13, 16, 17, 19, 21,
    22, 24-27, 31-33, 37, 39,
    42, 44, 49, 54, 55, 61,
    66, 71, 73, 76, 79-82,
    84-86, 89, 92, 95, 128,
    135, 145, 147, 149,
    151-153, 159, 160, 163
citadel 99
civil war 20, 119, 123
class 5, 39, 56, 60, 91, 107
classical authors 9, 43
clergy 16, 62, 92, 128, 131, 132
clerical 5, 14, 62, 91
combat 100
commentary(ies) 13, 33, 41, 66,
    72, 74-78, 80-86, 91,
    101, 109, 157, 158
commonwealth 55
community(ies) 2, 5, 13, 16, 18,
    19, 37, 40, 42, 44, 49,
    50, 54, 55, 60, 87, 100,
    129, 144
companion(s) 5, 43, 62, 63,
    80, 96, 97, 99, 100, 115,
    122, 134, 137, 138, 139,
    143
compassion 78, 107, 108,
    115, 148
concordance 70
confession(s) 61, 85, 108, 131,
    138, 154
confidence 22, 27, 116, 125, 142
conscience 98, 125, 132, 142,
    144
console 107
contemplation 103, 104
contempt 83
corruption 112
cosmos 40, 130
counsel(s) 35, 63, 91, 103, 106,
    112, 122, 133-138, 144
counsellor 133
court(s) 5, 6, 11, 12, 21, 61, 62,
    104, 110, 118, 120, 122,
    124, 126, 127, 135,
    142-144, 156
court system 110

court theologians 5, 6, 62, 135
creation 1, 40, 47, 48, 56, 57,
84, 106, 113, 114, 129
credal formulae 70
creed 43
cross 51, 132
crumbs 47, 72, 73, 76, 79, 84,
87, 89-91, 145, 146, 153
dead, death 10-12, 18, 20, 40,
46, 48, 51, 57, 76, 77,
78, 117, 127, 149
discernment 71, 95, 120, 141,
154
discipline(s) 1, 2, 4, 14, 74, 118,
144
discretio 38
divine 7, 22, 38, 40, 45, 47, 48,
50, 53, 58, 65, 67, 68,
78, 79, 86, 89, 90, 91,
113, 118, 121, 125, 129,
134-136, 141, 143, 145
doctores sacres 42
doctrine(s) 3, 4, 6, 24-26, 37, 38,
42, 44, 63
dog(s) 72, 73, 76, 77-85, 87, 89,
91, 98, 145, 149, 152,
153
dominion 57
dove 96
doxology 92
dust and ashes 20
dynastic wars 12, 117, 121
ecclesiastical 24, 25, 33, 61
Ecclesiastics 128
edition(s) 4, 13, 35, 67, 75, 147,
157, 158, 162
educate, educated, education 9,
16, 18, 19, 26, 29-31,
35, 44, 86, 93, 159
eight 99, 105, 106, 108, 155
elders 107, 137
elitism 74

enemy(ies) 78, 84, 85, 97, 99
127, 128, 153
envy, envious 94-96, 112, 123,
139, 142, 155
episcopacy 42
episcopal 14, 16, 104, 116
eschatological 49, 139, 141
eternal 59, 78, 92, 105, 111,
113, 139
ethic(s), ethical 38, 5, 127, 135
ethnic 84, 85
etymology 45, 87
eucharistic 14, 37, 66, 76
eucharistic controversy 37
evangelist 148, 151
evil companions 96, 100, 122,
138
evil powers 73
exegesis 3, 5, 7, 39, 40, 42-45,
50, 65, 69, 72, 74, 86,
92, 94, 101, 105, 158,
161, 162
exegetes 2, 3, 40, 42, 45, 70
exegetical chain 34, 66
exhortation 97, 110, 141, 142
exorcism 85, 91
experience(s) 5, 7, 22, 38, 40,
41, 49-52, 64, 95, 106,
109, 116, 161
exposition 24, 40, 56, 75, 77, 79,
81, 85, 86, 88-90, 91,
93, 119
factions 122, 124, 128
faith 7, 1, 2, 43, 44, 48, 49,
53-56, 59, 62, 67, 71-74,
76, 79, 80-82, 85, 86,
128, 136, 137, 142, 144,
147, 149, 150, 151,
152-154, 159
faith communities 44
family(ies) 5, 9-11, 14, 15, 20,
21, 48, 96, 111, 114,

115, 117, 125, 127, 137, 139, 143 , 158, 160
father 9, 12, 79, 93, 117-122, 124, 127, 139, 141, 149, 150, 152
fear of the Lord 102, 106-108
feast(s) 50, 62, 67
feminist 1, 4, 7, 8, 77
feudal 19, 56, 58, 117-119, 121, 124-127, 131, 133, 134, 141, 142
feudal hierarchy 118, 119, 127, 131
feudal lord 56, 117-119, 124
fifteen 105, 155
fight, fighting 97-99, 127, 144
figura 45
filial 120, 122, 123, 133, 139, 142
filial obedience 122, 123, 142
fire 115, 136, 138
florilegia 31
food 26, 82, 132, 133, 152
forgive, forgiveness 115, 131, 141
fornication 77, 97
fortitude 103, 105, 123
fortune(s) 12, 13, 20, 21, 56, 96, 114. 137
Frankish world 125, 141
friend(s) 1, 7, 76, 98
fruitful, fruitfulness 3, 111
fuller sense 45
funeral 18
Gaul 82
gems 113
genealogical 28
generosity 90, 94, 107, 112, 113, 115, 130
genre 21, 32-34, 93
Gentile(s) 73, 77, 78, 79-81, 83, 91, 148, 150-154

geography 13, 72, 75, 162
Germanic tribes 83
gift(s) 12, 17, 21, 22, 23, 26, 76, 78, 88, 93-95, 99-108, 121, 148, 155
gift of counsel 103
gifts of the Holy Spirit 26, 93-95, 99, 100, 102, 105, 155
glossaries 31
gold 16, 113, 136, 138
goldsmith 135, 138
good companions 137, 138
good deeds 85, 153
good works 26, 100, 128, 151, 156
goods 53, 103, 113, 130
Gospel(s) 26, 33, 52, 55, 60, 61, 66, 67, 68, 74-76, 79, 80, 83, 86, 88, 89, 91, 148, 160
grace 101, 104, 114, 139, 151
grammarians 31
greed 111, 112, 116
handbook(s) 21, 27, 28, 36, 45, 64
harts 47, 129
hawks 96
Hebrew 18
heretical 42
hermeneutic 5, 41, 48, 52, 53, 65, 70
hermeneutical circle 53
hierarchy 62, 93, 103, 117-119, 125, 127, 131, 141
historical 5, 1-3, 6, 9, 13, 20, 21, 32, 40, 43, 44, 46, 47, 49, 50, 65, 74-77, 81, 82, 84, 95, 109, 119, 124, 133, 139, 158, 159, 162
history 3, 2-5, 8, 12, 13, 16, 21, 32, 34, 35, 40, 41, 43,

44, 46, 47-50, 52, 55,
56, 72, 79, 82, 84, 93,
114, 123, 134, 135, 142,
160-163
historical interpretation 83
holiness 41, 104, 105, 116
Holy Spirit 26, 93-95, 99-102,
105, 107, 155
homiletic 33, 39, 67
homilary(ies) 31, 33, 34, 39, 66,
74
hope 8, 53, 57, 59, 63, 82, 139,
153
hospitality 19, 107, 108
host(s) 79, 153
hostage 12, 117
house of God 82
humility 20, 62, 76, 79, 82, 102,
108, 127, 149, 152, 153
hungry 63, 132, 133
iconoclasm 37
idolatry 143, 149
illiterate 112
imagery 26
images 28, 46, 58, 76, 90, 91
imagination 18, 41, 44, 58, 76,
109
imperial policy 39
indigence 114
inferiors, inferior ranks 93,
129
inheritance 11, 12, 49, 104
instruction(s) 1, 25, 34, 61, 66,
95, 97, 113
intellectual 18, 29, 32, 34, 52,
58, 71, 74, 88
interpret 42, 46, 56, 143, 153
interpretation 4, 6, 8, 24-27, 38,
41-47, 49, 52-56, 65-67,
72, 73, 74, 76, 77, 80,
81, 83, 84, 86, 93, 94,
104, 108, 109
intimacy with God 98, 137

Israel 43, 44, 49, 73, 78-81, 83,
122, 124, 139, 143, 148,
149, 152
Jesus 49, 73, 74, 77-81, 83, 86,
122, 147, 148
Jew(s) 14, 17, 18, 44, 45, 73, 82,
83, 92, 124, 152
journey 20, 60, 61, 81, 82, 104,
150, 151
judgment(s) 113, 120, 144
justification 20, 24-26, 45, 62,
65, 85, 87, 89
kin 17, 137
king(s) 10, 16, 19, 48, 49, 57,
117, 118, 123, 124, 127,
128, 134, 135, 137, 143
King's relatives 118
Kingdom of God 59, 60, 98, 104,
106, 124, 137
kingdom of Israel 122
kingship theory 135
knight(s) 28, 60, 100, 117, 118,
128, 133, 139, 141, 144,
155
laity 14, 32, 33, 65, 92
lay, layman, laywoman,
laywomen 5, 8, 30,
31, 66, 69, 92, 109,
116
Latin 9, 34-35, 42, 65, 66, 69,
72, 75, 77, 85, 100, 132,
147, 150
law 22, 24, 48, 144
leaders 5, 95, 107, 127, 136
learn, learned, learning 9, 18,
28-30, 43, 52, 73, 92,
99, 100, 101, 103, 108,
109, 112, 126, 127, 129,
133, 137, 151, 161
lectio divina 53, 66, 68, 71, 72,
74, 92, 108
lectionary(ies) 33, 66, 67, 68,
160, 163

legislation 22, 24, 25
letter(s) 35, 39, 76, 77, 85, 87, 153
liberation theology 1
library(ies) 3, 7, 30-33, 35, 74
likeness to God 103
litanies 61
literacy 29, 30, 39, 165
literary 4, 6, 9, 15, 19, 21, 27, 28, 30, 32, 33, 87, 109, 119, 161
literary form 28
literary structure 109
liturgical 3, 5, 22, 32-34, 39, 40, 49-51, 61, 62, 66-68, 74, 91, 160
liturgical context 49, 50, 66, 68
liturgy(ies) 49-52, 61, 67, 68, 158, 160
liturgy of the hours 61
loaves 72, 73
logion 78, 84
lord(s) 12, 47, 56, 57, 63, 66, 89, 92, 101, 102, 106-108, 111, 117-119, 124-127, 130, 132, 133, 136, 138, 142, 143, 148, 149, 150-153, 156, 157
lowliness 102
loyalty(ies) 5, 6, 117, 121, 124, 127, 128, 141, 142
lust 94, 96, 97, 142
magnate 93, 110, 112
Magnificat 63
manuscript(s) 7, 4, 16, 34-36, 39, 66
marriage 10, 11, 28, 60, 87, 97
Mary, Virgin 62, 63
mass(es) 15, 51, 61, 68, 160
master(s) 11, 39, 43, 79, 97, 116, 130, 145
material possessions 111-113, 123
maternal vocation 93

meaning(s) 1, 3, 7, 23, 26, 27, 40-47, 51, 53, 54, 67, 70-72, 75-77, 79, 81, 83-85, 89, 90, 94, 129
meditation, meditative 34, 51, 52, 66, 92
meekness, meek 102, 103, 109, 111, 156
memorization 70
metaphor, metaphoric 18, 57, 60, 100, 135, 136, 139
metonymy 82, 89
mildness 98
military skills 105
ministers 66, 91, 145
ministry 22, 77, 83, 130, 160
mirror(s) 7, 17, 21, 27, 28, 45
missionaries 81
model(s) 33, 34, 47, 48, 51, 52, 79, 88, 92, 98, 102, 119, 121, 123, 125, 127, 128, 130, 137, 139, 142, 143, 161
monastery(ies), monastic 1, 5, 10, 12, 14, 16, 17, 31, 32, 35, 39, 41, 50, 51, 54, 70-72, 80, 85, 90, 92, 94, 95, 98, 100, 108, 161
monks 33, 54, 85, 97, 100
moral ambiguity 117, 118
moral code(s) 28, 71
mourning 11, 103, 109
mystery(ies) 4, 6, 7, 40, 42, 43, 50-52, 55, 57, 61, 78, 85, 88, 90, 148, 153
mystical 22, 40, 81, 82, 84, 88, 153
narratives 49, 67, 122, 133
nation(s) 48, 81, 82, 83, 84, 148, 149, 151, 152
needy 61, 115
neo-Platonic 43, 44

New Testament 6, 43, 70, 109, 124, 129, 130, 142, 157
Nîmes 4, 13, 34, 35, 159
nobility 9, 18, 56, 60, 96, 117, 118, 125, 127, 128, 133, 159
nourishment 26, 67, 149, 152
number symbolism, numerology 45, 47, 101, 105
obedience 5, 117, 120-123, 125, 134, 141-143, 153
obligation(s) 9, 88, 107, 113, 117-121, 124, 125, 127 128, 131, 133, 136, 141, 142
offering(s) 25, 138
oil 46, 111, 131
Old Testament 44, 45, 47-49, 58, 115, 122-124, 130, 135-137, 142
order(s) 2, 6, 7, 17, 37, 38, 48, 74, 78, 80, 81, 85, 102-108, 114, 117, 118-120, 131, 134, 138, 141, 142, 145, 147, 149, 151, 152
orthodox, orthodoxy 6, 37, 42, 43, 56, 58, 72
ownership 55-57, 113
pagan(s) 45, 76, 78, 137, 149, 152
parable 78, 79, 83, 148
parallel 46, 47, 65, 67, 72, 81, 84, 88, 101, 102, 105, 106, 121, 135
passion(s) 31, 62, 63, 73, 144, 148
pastoral 29, 37-39, 62, 92
pastoral theology 38
patience 7, 76, 79, 82, 83, 94, 98, 127, 149, 152
Patristic 33, 39, 40, 43, 45, 46, 63, 65, 160, 161, 163

peace 15, 60, 61, 84, 90, 93, 96, 102-104, 107, 128, 139, 153
pedagogical 26, 47, 69
Pentateuch 123
perception 27, 143, 158
perfection 53, 57, 60, 61, 94, 98, 100-102, 106, 111, 134, 138
pericope 66-69, 74, 77, 81, 83, 90
pharisees 77, 80, 147, 150
pietas 15
piety 61, 102, 106, 107, 150, 151
pilgrims 115, 132, 133
political, politics 1, 3, 5, 6, 7, 14, 24, 28, 47, 55, 56, 69, 77, 106, 116, 117, 122, 123, 113, 133-135, 141, 143, 144
political theologies 1
poor, poverty 20, 55, 61, 107, 110, 112-116, 132, 155, 156
power 2, 18, 21, 25-27, 29, 40, 53, 56, 57, 61, 62, 73, 74, 85, 90, 104, 107, 110, 111, 113, 114, 120, 121, 125, 131, 142
practical theology 2, 3, 38, 71, 92, 109, 110
pragmatism 136, 143
praxis 2, 4, 52-54, 109
prayer(s) 22, 47, 51-53, 56, 61, 71, 82, 85, 88, 89, 91, 92, 93, 99, 107, 115, 119, 126-128, 130, 132, 137, 138, 143, 144, 149, 152
predestination 37
pride 35, 78, 94, 95, 148, 155
priest(s) 33, 47, 91, 92, 118, 131, 132

prince(s) 59, 93
proclamation 40
prophetic 55, 92, 142, 143
prosperity 106, 123, 137
providence 144
prudence 31, 96, 124, 126, 134,
      138
psalm(s) 18, 47, 67, 68, 70,
      90, 91, 109, 112
psychological 6
psychomachia 93, 94
punishment 106, 110
purity of heart 103
quiescence 104
rank(s)   9, 107, 118, 121,
      127-131, 139, 141, 156
rationale, rationality 72, 74, 119,
      125, 134
read(s), reading 7, 4, 5, 6, 9, 18,
      20, 23, 24, 28, 29, 32,
      33, 34, 38, 39, 41, 42,
      43-45, 50-53, 56, 61, 63,
      68, 69, 70, 72, 77, 80,
      87, 92, 106, 108, 109,
      112, 122, 125, 126, 132,
      142, 143, 155
realm 127, 131, 141
Redeemer 57, 130
reform(s) 18, 21, 29, 68, 95
repentance 122, 131, 141
responsorial(s) 67, 92, 126, 145
rhetorical 39, 45, 47
rich(es) 17, 19, 29, 41, 45, 55,
      92, 112, 113, 123
righteousness 81, 102-104
rituals 49
role(s) 6, 7, 20, 22, 24-27, 41,
      47, 54, 63, 65, 86, 88,
      112, 119, 128, 133, 134,
      136-139
Roman rite 67, 68, 160
royal counsellor 7, 56, 118, 119,
      130, 133, 134

sacrament(s), sacramental 24,
      49, 50, 61, 68, 131,
      144
sacrifice(s) 61, 76, 82
sacrifice of the mass 61
sadness 94, 127
saint(s) 10, 14, 39, 42, 60, 62,
      63, 69, 159
salvation 5-7, 40, 42, 44, 47-50,
      53, 56, 60, 61, 73, 78,
      82, 83, 122, 132, 134,
      135, 142, 148, 151, 152
savior 63,
school(s) 16, 32, 54
scribe(s) 69, 80, 85, 147, 150
scriptural curse 120
Scripture(s) 3, 5, 9, 34, 40-43,
      45, 50, 51, 52, 53, 58,
      63, 69, 71, 72, 84-86,
      88, 89, 92, 102, 103,
      106-109, 116, 125, 129,
      131, 136, 137, 142, 144,
      153, 154
self-identity 6
senses 45
serenity 104
serpent 96
service 11, 15, 56, 124-127, 130,
      143
seven 35, 93, 99, 102, 105,
      106, 158
sheep 78, 79, 83, 84, 148, 153
Sidon 73, 76, 78, 81, 147, 150
sin(s) 73, 82, 93, 97, 98, 100,
      103, 122, 128, 131, 132,
      158
sinfulness 20, 115
social action 61
social ideal 28
social order 7, 104, 107, 108,
      114, 117
social relationships 96, 107
social system 61

soldier(s) 99, 116, 125
son(s) 4, 5, 8-13, 17, 19, 21, 22,
    23, 25, 26, 34, 35, 38,
    47, 59, 63,   69, 82,
    87-89, 91, 96, 98, 99,
    105, 106, 111, 113,
    115-117, 120, 121, 122,
    123, 126, 127, 128, 131,
    139, 145, 147, 149, 152,
    158
soteriological purpose 38
soteriology 59, 129
source(s) 3, 1, 13, 29, 31, 42,
    46, 47, 58, 63, 67, 76,
    82, 92, 112, 121, 122,
    130, 131, 141, 147, 157,
    158, 162
sovereign, sovereignty 56, 57,
    127, 141
Spanish adoptionism 37
speculum 27-29, 45, 158, 162
spiritual 2, 3, 16, 21, 25, 26, 28,
    29, 33, 39, 40, 41, 46,
    49, 61, 63, 88, 91, 95,
    96, 98, 99, 100, 102,
    103, 104, 108, 118, 121,
    123, 124, 127, 136, 137,
    141, 142, 146
spiritual sense 40, 85, 153
spirituality 38, 106, 109, 119,
    136, 144
stability 103
state in life 98
stewardship 113, 114
strangers 115
strategy(ies) 6, 47, 97, 100, 106,
    118, 121, 136
struggles 14, 15, 61, 137
study(ies), studied, studying 3, 1,
    3, 5, 7, 22, 27, 29, 31,
    32, 35, 43, 44, 45, 53,
    55, 61, 66, 67, 68, 69,
    71, 87, 88, 91, 99, 102,

    103, 106, 108, 109, 115,
    126, 131, 144, 153, 159,
    160, 161, 162
suffer, suffering 134, 138
superior(s) 58, 93, 128, 129, 132
Syro-Phoenician woman 5, 47,
    65-69, 72-75, 77-79, 82,
    86, 87, 89, 145, 150
table 5, 19, 47, 66, 73, 84, 85,
    87, 89-91, 111, 131-133,
    145, 146, 149, 152, 153
teacher(s) 22, 24-27, 62, 65, 78,
    79, 83, 86, 88, 126, 133
temptation(s) 7, 94, 100, 122,
    123, 135, 155
theocracy, theocratic 5, 135,
    144
theological method 1, 3
theology 1-3, 5-8, 19, 37-39, 41,
    43, 44, 54, 55, 57, 60,
    69, 71, 76, 92, 109, 110,
    114, 116, 117, 129, 131,
    144, 162
theology of creation 114, 129
theoria 40
theory(ies) 2, 3, 22, 31, 56, 109,
    118, 135
topos 19, 21
tradition(s) 3, 6, 7, 13, 15,
    16, 18, 21, 22, 25-27,
    30, 34, 39-43, 50, 51,
    54, 57, 63-67, 70-72, 74,
    75, 86, 93-96, 99, 101,
    105, 108, 109, 113, 116,
    125, 161
transitory 59, 60, 113
translation(s) 4, 10, 35, 38, 68,
    69, 75, 81, 100, 101,
    121, 132
transmission 34, 65
treachery 122, 124, 125, 128
treaty, treatise(s) 17, 21, 34, 38,
    39, 55, 66, 71

treaty, treatise(s) 17, 21, 34, 38,
        39, 55, 66, 71
trinity 45, 52, 56, 58, 59, 131
truth 5, 59, 89, 96, 103, 115,
        129, 151
type(s) 43, 44, 46, 59, 73, 81,
        151
typology, typological 5, 6, 40,
        43-45, 47, 49, 50, 55,
        81, 160, 163
Tyre 73, 76, 78, 81, 147, 150
understanding 1, 3-8, 21,
        22, 25, 29, 39, 41, 44,
        47, 50-53, 55-61, 63, 70,
        73, 74, 77, 79-81, 84-86,
        88-92, 102, 103, 105,
        106, 109, 119, 126,
        134-136, 139, 142, 145,
        146
unworthiness 20, 25, 88
usury 55
Ùzes 9, 11, 13-19, 136, 158, 159
vice(s) 4, 28, 34, 77, 85, 93-97,
        98, 99, 100, 106, 108,
        112, 116, 139, 155
vigilance 96
virtue(s) 21, 28, 34, 53, 56, 58-
        60, 63, 73, 79, 81, 92,
        93-99, 106, 111, 112,
        116, 118, 126, 127, 132,
        134, 137, 138, 139, 144,
        155
vocation 7, 24, 38, 93, 99, 119,
        127, 134, 135, 143
Vulgate 8, 77
war(s) 12, 20, 94-97, 100, 117,
        121

war of the virtues and vices 95
warfare 19, 98-100
warrior(s) 6, 28, 89, 98, 102,
        116, 133
water 13, 44, 115
weak 20, 22, 57, 61, 103, 130
wealth, wealthy 55, 61, 113, 116,
        132
wickedness 73
will of God 69, 88, 127, 130
wine 111, 131
wisdom, wise 5, 15, 18, 19,
        22, 24, 29, 34, 41, 42,
        45, 47, 49, 63, 65, 66,
        67, 71, 86, 88, 89, 91,
        92, 101-104, 106, 108,
        109, 117, 120-124, 126,
        129, 134-137, 139, 142,
        143
woman, women 3, 4, 5, 7-10, 20,
        22, 24-26, 36, 47, 65-69,
        72-79, 81-83, 85, 86, 88,
        89, 91, 145, 147-149,
        150-153, 159-161, 163
worship 49, 158
write(s), writer(s) 3-5, 7, 9, 21-
        24, 32, 42, 43, 48, 52,
        54, 63, 66, 74, 75, 81,
        86, 87, 93, 95, 101, 112,
        113, 131, 117, 137, 159
young, younger, youth 6, 79, 89,
        93, 96, 98, 107, 111,
        116, 133, 136, 137